The Mother/Daughter Connection

the Mother/Daughter CONNECTION

by Susie Shellenberger

WORD PUBLISHING

NASHVILLE

A Thomas Nelson Company

Dedicated to

Kathy and Kelly Gowler, whose own

mother/daughter connection is filled with

laughter, trust, love,

and Christ.

I'm ready for girls' night out any time you are.

Love you both,

Susie

C ontents

Introduction   xi

1. I Don't Understand My Body!   1
   Mom's Survival Kit: Stuff You Gotta Know!
   Give Your Daughter the Right Heroes   25

2. Preteen to Teen: Making the Transition Easier   30
   Mom's Survival Kit: Stuff You Gotta Know!
   Is Your Home a Safe Haven?   55

3. Eating Disorders: They Can Eat You Alive!   58
   Mom's Survival Kit: Stuff You Gotta Know!
   What's the Problem? Take It to Christ!   89

4. Classroom Challenges   93
   Mom's Survival Kit: Stuff You Gotta Know!
   Teaching Your Daughter about Lordship   109

5. Classroom Debates   113
   Mom's Survival Kit: Stuff You Gotta Know!
   Handling the Cash   130

6. Sexual Purity   134
    Mom's Survival Kit: Stuff You Gotta Know!
    Friends Are Friends Forever?   171

7. Communication   175
    Mom's Survival Kit: Stuff You Gotta Know!
    The Opposite Sex . . . and Your DAUGHTER!   194

8. Giving Your Daughter a Spiritual Heritage   198
    Mom's Survival Kit: Stuff You Gotta Know!
    Building Your Daughter's Confidence   211

9. Guiding Your Post-Teen Daughter   214
    Mom's Survival Kit: Stuff You Gotta Know!
    Shaping a Servant   226

Conclusion   231

Endnotes   233

About the Author   235

$\mathcal{I}$ntroduction

It's been said that every war gives birth to a song. Remember the mix of artists who united during Desert Storm to record the song that promised soldiers that when they went to sleep at night all of America would be praying for them?

And flashing even further back . . . remember the song born out of the Vietnam War, "Where Have All the Flowers Gone?"

Catchy tune.

Smooth rhythm.

Haunting lyrics.

Makes me want to rewrite the words and sing, "Where Have All the Families Gone?" Is it just me, or wasn't there a time when families actually pulled together—you know, like a team? For many today, that's simply an outdated script played out on reruns of *Little House on the Prairie*, *The Brady Bunch*, or *The Waltons*.

Hmmm. Could it be that Charles and Caroline, Mike and Carol, and John and Olivia knew something that we've forgotten?

Think about it: They said goodnight to their kids. They had meals together. They gave hugs. Victories—like making the spelling bee or reciting lines in the Christmas pageant—were turned into family celebrations. And disappointments—such as not making the team or getting the chicken pox—were made bearable by family empathy.

It seems somewhere down the line we've lost the value of *family*. Granted, our high-tech society speeding down the information superhighway will never return to a slower, simpler lifestyle. But we *can* recapture some of the ingredients, such as character, integrity, and old-fashioned values, that made families of the past a *team*.

How do you recapture those ingredients?

They're found through simple, yet priceless, truths. One of the most valuable lessons I learned as a child was to ask, "Will you forgive me?" when I hurt someone's feelings. I learned it easily because my parents modeled it for me. They were quick to seek *my* forgiveness at times and expected me to do the same.

I have adult Christian friends who have never uttered the words, "Will you forgive me?" Yes, they've said "I'm sorry" from time to time. But there's something especially humbling about seeking forgiveness.

What would happen if you asked your daughter to forgive you for breaking a promise, overreacting, getting angry, or jumping to conclusions before hearing her side?

Spending time together is another golden ingredient in family unity. I remember Mom cooking popcorn flavored in bacon grease on top of the stove so we'd have something special to munch on during a game of Sorry, Trouble, or Chinese Checkers. Time together doesn't have to cost a lot of money, but it *will* require commitment. We prayed together regularly. Church wasn't an option—if the doors were open, we were there. And once-a-year vacations were a priority we carefully budgeted a year in advance. We enjoyed family traditions.

What would happen, Mom, if you started spending quality time with your daughter on a regular basis—just the two of you?

How would your daughter react if you tucked her in tonight? Hugged her tomorrow morning? Slipped an "I love you" note in her wallet? Or allowed yourself to cry in front of her . . . and with her?

I'm guessing that if you pulled some of these ingredients

together, your mother/daughter relationship would actually begin to connect in a powerful and healing way.

Mom, God has assigned you the most important job in the world! It's your privilege—with His help—to guide your daughter through her childhood and teen years so she can become a godly young lady who will glorify her heavenly Father.

Your work is cut out for you! But, guess what—you're not alone. Let's join hands and raise up a generation of godly women!

C'mon! I'll meet you inside the pages.

—Susie Shellenberger
Colorado Springs, Colorado

I Don't Understand My Body!

Dear Diary:

I can't believe it! Today at lunch, Jessica told me she got her period last night. Part of me is all, "Yuuuuuck!" And the other part of me is like, "So when's mine coming?"

We're only eleven. I thought it didn't happen till you were like, you know, a teen. After Jessica was bragging about it—thinking she's all that because it happened—Shawni said she heard our class is gonna have one of those health thingees soon, and we'll all havta learn about it.

I guess I'm kinda excited. In a way. But I'm also kinda scared. I mean . . . gag! Who wants to bleed every month? But Jessica says it means she's a real woman now. Oh, gimme a break!

Mom's calling me to supper. Later.

Dear Diary:

Shawni was right. Today's the day for "the talk." You know . . . all that stuff about our bodies and all those changes and stuff. All the guys gotta go to the cafeteria, and the girls are hanging around the library to watch some film.

Like wake me up when it's over, K?

Aaron has on a new shirt. He's gorgeous. I wonder if he even knows my name?

Aaron   AaRoN   AARON

AARON AND ME 4-EVER

Later . . .

Diary:

K, the film wasn't as stupid as I thought it was gonna be, but who cares about all that ovulation gunk? All I wanna know is the important stuff. Like . . . you know . . .

When am I gonna get my period?

WHAT'S THE DIFFERENCE BETWEEN TAMPONS AND PADS? AND WHICH ONES SHOULD I USE?

DOES IT HURT TO USE TAMPONS?

Can I still take a shower when I'm having my period?

WHAT IF I'M CRAMPING SO BAD I THINK I'M GONNA EXPLODE INTO THE NEXT AREA CODE?

Dear Diary:

Our health class is having a nurse come tomorrow. She's supposed to answer all our questions about all this stuff. I'm so sure! There's no way. I mean, there is totally no way I would ever in a ~~thousand hundred million bazillion~~ gazillion years EVER ask some of the questions I have OUT LOUD in front of THE WHOLE PLANET!

I'd die first.

I really would.

I really really really truly would.

But it sure would feel good to know the answers. I wonder how I'll ever know . . . if I don't ask, I mean.

Wish there were someone I could talk to without feeling so weird.

Eric and David just walked by. Eric and David. Eric and David and me. Eric and David are totally fine.

Gotta go. Aaron's coming!

Come On, Mom . . . Be That Person!

Like all girls, your preteen daughter is wishing she could have her questions answered without feeling embarrassed. It's doubtful she'll share those questions with the school nurse or a special speaker in her health class. The risk of embarrassment is too great.

Since she's needing someone . . . wouldn't it be great (okay, perfect!) if *you* were that someone! Come on, Mom—take the initiative.

Instead of making her approach *you* with her questions, start the process before she even *has* questions. Think about it: If you and your daughter are talking about intimate things before she's eleven years old, it's going to seem natural to *continue* discussing these subjects when she's a teenager.

"I wish my mom wouldn't always ask to help me with my homework. I want to try and figure it out first."

Kelly, fifteen

Maybe you're just now realizing the necessity of a close relationship with your daughter. There's no time like the present to get started! Make an effort to spend some quality one-on-one time with her to let her know that she can ask you anything. Here are a few suggestions to get you started.

Dating Your Daughter

Make it a priority to reserve a specific time each week (or every other week, depending on schedules) simply to be with your daughter. No interruptions. No other people. No agenda. Just you and her. It doesn't have to be an expensive evening together nor even an entire evening.

Kathy and Kelly have a special weekly arrangement: Kathy meets her fourteen-year-old daughter at the front of the school every Thursday, checks her out for forty minutes during the lunch hour, and takes her to Taco Bell.

Kelly looks forward to their weekly date. This gives mom and daughter a chance to catch up during the middle of a school day in the middle of a hectic week.

Of course, if this were the *only* time they spent together, it wouldn't count for much. But Kathy has made this an extra event for Kelly to look forward to.

After Libby finishes her weekly guitar lesson, Martha treats her to a burger, fries, and a cherry Dr. Pepper at Sonic's drive-through. It's a weekly tradition for them.

Tuck-Ins

There's something special about being tucked in at night, isn't there? It brings security. Closure. After a rough day at school, peer pressure, being snubbed by a guy . . . your daughter *needs* a tuck-in even if she won't admit it.

Lois has a nightly routine: She sits on the edge of Leslie's bed every night, pulls the covers up to her daughter's chin, and leans down and kisses her on the forehead.

This gives Lois a chance to help her daughter feel loved and secure after surviving another day in the "blackboard jungle." It also gives her an opportunity to ask some important questions:

- "What was the best thing that happened at school today?"
- "What was the worst thing that happened at school today?"
- "Were any of the other kids talking about stuff you didn't understand?"
- "Got any questions you want to ask me?"

And if Leslie's empty on questions, sometimes Lois prompts her:

- "Leslie, you're ten years old now. In a couple of years or so, you'll be starting your menstrual cycle—you know, your period. Some of your girlfriends will start way before you, and some of them will start a few years after you. And as you hear them talking about it, you might have a couple of questions. Guess what? I know all about periods. I've been having mine for a long time. And when you *do* have a question, you can ask me, okay?"

- "Leslie, do you know what it means to have the cramps?"

- "A tampon or a pad is kind of like wearing a Band-Aid while your body cleans itself out every month. Do you know the difference between a tampon and a pad?"

I believe that every girl in the world ought to have *someone* with whom she can talk about *anything*. No question is off-limits. No topic is too embarrassing. No word is too dirty. And, ideally, that *someone* should be her mom.

Think about it: When your first-grade daughter sees the f-word graffitied somewhere on the playground or the side of a building, it's likely she's going to ask *someone* what it means. Wouldn't it be great if *you*, Mom, were the someone? After all, you know her better than anyone. Therefore, you can discern how much information your six-year-old daughter can handle.

The more effort you put into establishing an intimate relation-

"So I don't make my bed. Is that really such a huge deal?"

Krista, fifteen

ship with your daughter, the easier it will be for her to come to *you* during her preteen and teenage years with the questions you'd rather answer yourself than leave to middle-school hallway gossip.

Mom's Refresher Course

Since it's been awhile since you started your menstrual cycle, perhaps you've forgotten about the all-important issues and questions preteen girls struggle with. Having a monthly period is a piece of cake for you. But for your preteen daughter who's still trying to understand what it *is*, it can be a nightmare waiting to happen.

So . . . let's go through the basics. You know, just so you'll be reminded of what's really going on inside her body when she starts asking the specifics. Face it, Mom—it's been awhile since you've had to stop and think through why and how your body works.

Oh, Yeah! I Remember Now

So you can be better equipped to answer your daughter's questions about her changing body, I encourage you to find an entire book devoted to the topic. A great general all-purpose book for women is *1250 Health-Care Questions Women Ask with Straight-forward Answers by an Obstetrician/Gynecologist.*[1]

Meanwhile, let's simply review some of the basics until you get around to purchasing an in-depth study on the female body. Though physical female development is nothing to be frightened of, many preteens *are* scared because they don't know what to expect. And that's where you come in, Mom. The better informed you are, the more confident you'll feel in equipping your daughter with the knowledge she needs and wants.

First Things First

As your daughter begins the process of becoming a young woman, one of the earliest signs she'll notice is the growth of hair under her arms and around her vaginal opening. Next, she'll notice that her hips are getting a little larger and her breasts are beginning to grow.

Can you remember what you were thinking and feeling during this time of your life? I receive about a thousand letters a month—as well as hundreds of e-mails. As you can imagine, those letters contain questions about everything from A to Z. Based on what I hear from preteen and teen girls, let me remind you what your daughter is probably thinking and feeling.

Something's wrong with me—my breast area is really sore. That's okay. She's in the process of physical development. Her breasts are beginning to grow.

I must be a freak! My right breast has started to grow, but my left one is still flat as a pancake. Assure her that she's normal. During breast development, both breasts do not grow at exactly the same rate. One usually always grows a little faster than the other one. Assure her that eventually, she *will* even out.

I can't believe I'm getting so fat! My hips are bigger. I'm gonna stop eating. Everyone probably thinks I'm way overweight. Let your daughter know that there's a reason her hips are getting a bit bigger; it's all part of God's plan for her body. Explain that He designed women's hips to be larger generally than men's to help her carry a baby and to aid her during the birth process.

What's happening to me? How come everything is changing? Teach your daughter that these physical changes are normal and that every girl in the world experiences these "growing pains." Explain that as long as she knows what's happening and *why* it's happening, there's absolutely nothing to be afraid of. As her mother, you'll want to warn her ahead of time what's going to happen, so she won't be caught off-guard.

I don't know what's the matter with me. Two of my friends have already started their periods, and I haven't. I'll probably never be able to have babies! Help your daughter understand that soon after her breasts begin to develop, her period probably won't be far away. Talk about tampons and pads. Make sure she knows how to use them. A wise mom will provide a feminine stash for her daughter in a special drawer in the bathroom and advise her to pack a pad in her purse or backpack just in case she begins her menstrual cycle when she's away from home. Showing your daughter how to be prepared for her period *before* it happens will alleviate her fear and apprehension about what to do when it does happen.

The Menstrual Cycle

As you know, the menstrual cycle is God's design to prepare a girl's body to give birth someday. Your daughter may become grumpy and edgy before her period actually begins. She may also have some cramping. This is because her hormones are going through a variety of changes that will cause her menstrual cycle to begin.

She may also notice a clear or whitish discharge on her underpants. This is normal—but it's also normal if she *doesn't* have any discharge.

When her period *does* begin, blood will pass from the uterus through the cervix and vagina. Some girls experience a heavier blood flow than others, but most will notice a lighter flow the third and fourth days.

It might be hard for you to remember your first period, but it's likely you were a little irregular at first. Explain to your daughter that this is normal. Her period will last anywhere from three to six days, and it will probably vary from month to month for a while. For instance, she may experience a light flow one month and a heavier flow the following month. She may also skip a month. As you know, stress, health, and other variables can all affect her menstrual cycle. Most women, however, have a cycle of approximately twenty-eight days. As your daughter gets older, her period will become more regulated.

The Basics 101

Okay, Mom. There are a few more basics your daughter is tossing around in her mind. Here's a heads-up: She may be struggling with how to ask you these questions, and she may not even be able to verbalize them yet. Why not approach her . . . instead of waiting for her to figure out how to ask?

What's ovulation? It's when the ovary releases an egg. The female body then begins preparing the inside of the uterus to nourish a baby in the event the egg becomes fertilized by a sperm and a child is conceived. When the body realizes it's not pregnant, it releases the blood and extra tissue it had previously stored for the baby. This is having a period. When we actually sit down and think about all the female body is doing on a monthly basis, it truly is amazing! Help your daughter see the menstrual cycle as a God-given, miraculous plan to prepare for a new life . . . instead of a monthly curse.

I've heard horror stories from older girls who say you bleed and bleed and bleed, and it's so much blood that it gets all over your underwear and clothes and even on your bedsheets. This scares me! The average woman loses two to eight tablespoons of blood every menstrual cycle (yet it always seems like more!). Assure your daughter that if she changes her pads or tampons frequently, she won't need to be frightened. The goal, of course, is to change her pad or tampon before she actually needs to, to prevent leaking onto her underwear. During especially heavy days, she may need to wear a tampon *and* a pad.

Will guys be able to tell when I'm on my period? No. No one will be able to "see" if she's menstruating or not. However, wearing really tight jeans *could* enable people to see the bulkiness of a pad through them. Again, she should change often and wear comfortable clothing.

I don't know if I should wear tampons or pads. Is your daughter active? If she's involved in sports, she may want to use tampons simply because of the convenience. If she's nervous about having her period, it's probably a good idea to start her off on pads. But make sure she knows about—and understands—both tampons *and* pads, and allow her to make the decision.

If I wear pads, can I wear them in the swimming pool? No. It would probably feel like wearing a wet diaper, and there's a good chance that some of the blood will leak into the pool. If she doesn't want to wear tampons, advise her not to swim during her period.

I overheard some older girls talking about how stinky their periods are. What if I smell bad and people make fun of me? Believe it or not, I've received letters from teen girls saying, "Susie, my mom told me if I took a bath during my period, I'd get really sick and maybe even die." I'd love to make some personal phone calls and ask those moms what planet their education came from!

Teach your daughter that good hygiene is *always* important—whether she's having a period or not. Most girls take a bath or shower every day. During her period, however, she may feel more confident taking a bath or shower in the morning *and* in the evening. Remember, she'll be self-conscious at first. Do everything you can to help her feel more relaxed and okay about herself. If she wants to take *three* baths a day, let her! In fact, surprise her with some special bubble bath or body wash to help her feel special.

I've heard that you get reallyreallyreally bad cramps during your period. Is this true? Some women experience severe cramping, and others don't notice any discomfort at all. What will help? Light exercising (because it relaxes the muscles) and an over-the-counter painkiller that contains ibuprofen (Advil, Motrin, Nuprin, Medipren). If these don't help, consider asking your doctor to prescribe something stronger. I've used Anaprox and extra-strength Motrin, and both have helped.

I'm scared about having to take gym next year at school. I'm afraid to take a shower in front of other girls. They might make fun of my body. Real friends don't make each other uncomfortable. Usually people who are poking fun at others are insecure and trying to make themselves look better. They believe if they can make someone else look less than average, *they* will look above average. This is something we'll all deal with for the rest of our lives.

Help your daughter understand that in school—and someday in the workplace—there will always be an insecure individual who will strive to build him- or herself up by tearing someone else down.

Some school gyms have shower stalls with curtains; some don't. If your daughter is nervous about having to shower in front of other girls, help her prepare ahead of time. Together, create a duffel bag of things to make her feel more comfortable—an extra-long towel (many department stores sell a "Big Towel") or a beach towel, and all the accessories she'll need (deodorant, brush, perfume, soap, washcloth) so she can grab them in a split second. This will cut down on time spent standing in the nude and fumbling around for something she needs. Then remind her that PE class won't last forever—it *will* come to an end!

I'm afraid I'll start my period when I'm at school. I'll die! This is a major fear of preteen girls. They envision walking down the hall with blood all over their clothes and being made fun of the rest of their lives. Again, the key is to help your daughter be prepared. The more prepared she is (having a pad or tampon with her and knowing how to use it), the less she'll fear the unknown.

I keep hearing the term PMS. What is it? Premenstrual syndrome is caused by the fluctuation of our hormones. Some women become angry; others cry easily. Your daughter may want to refrain from drinking caffeine a few days before and during her period. You may also want to advise your daughter to steer clear of making any major decisions during this time (switching a class, changing friends, dropping out of the school play, etc.).

When am I going to start my period? Almost all my friends already have theirs! Mom, when did your menstrual cycle begin? Oftentimes, your daughter will begin her period around the same age you started. Volunteer this information. Tell her everything you can remember—including some of the fears you used to have. You may also want to share (and laugh about) some of the

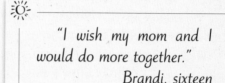

"I wish my mom and I would do more together."
Brandi, sixteen

inconveniences women had to go through in the past (sanitary belts, nonadhesive pads, etc.).

I heard if I use a tampon, I'm not a virgin anymore. I get several letters each year from girls who are worried about losing their virginity from tampon use. Please teach your daughter that a tampon is simply a piece of feminine protection—a "Band-Aid" to catch the blood flow from her body. This has absolutely nothing to do with sexual purity or being a virgin.

Does it hurt to use a tampon? How do I get it in? The school nurse gave a free sample box to all the fifth-grade girls, but I don't understand the diagram on the paper inside. This is one of the most frequently asked questions by preteen and teen girls. As adults, most of us take for granted the ease with which we use tampons. But to an eleven- or twelve-year-old girl, it's still a foreign object.

To help remind you of your daughter's mindset—and to encourage you to pass this information along to her—I'm including an article I asked a friend of mine to write. Nancy Rue is a full-time writer with several fiction books to her credit. You'll enjoy her piece on tampons.

TamPon TrouBles
BY NANCY N. RUE

*Everything You've Always Wanted to Know **about Tampons**—and **Weren't** Afraid to Ask!*

We've been getting a lot of letters at *Brio* magazine recently from girls who are feeling somewhat "tampon challenged." Let's take a few minutes to answer your questions and set your mind at ease, okay?

Maybe you've been wondering . . .

"Are tampons okay to use—even if you're a virgin?"

"When is it okay to start using them?"

"I'm having trouble getting it in."

"It's so uncomfortable!"

"What about toxic shock syndrome?"

You're Okay!

It's a strange thing. Having your period when you're a teenager is as natural as craving junk food. It's a big part of your being able to have babies someday (you've undoubtedly heard all the stuff about the eggs popping out every month), so it's definitely something that you, as a young woman, *want* to have happening. But even though it's perfectly normal and wonderful, we sure don't like to talk about it. Well, blush no more! You've obviously heard that tampons are one way to make the whole period hassle easier, and you're right. Read on, and we'll try to answer some of those questions for you.

What's a Tampon, and How Does It Work?

In case you've never actually seen one, a tampon is a narrow tube of absorbent cotton designed to be inserted into the vagina. Because your vagina is very flexible, the cotton molds itself to it and absorbs the blood during your menstrual period. Like a sponge, a tampon becomes larger as it takes on fluid.

A tampon definitely has advantages over a pad. If it's in right, you can't feel a thing—unlike when you're wearing a miniature mattress! A tampon is small enough that you can carry a supply in your purse for emergencies. And because it's worn *internally*, there's less chance of odor. Most girls love tampons because they can be worn with a swimsuit or gymnastics garb and never be seen. You can even wear them in the pool!

Tampons come in various shapes and sizes, just as there are different shapes and sizes of female bodies. It's a good idea to "collect" a variety of tampons—cardboard applicators, slim fits, plastic applicators—and experiment with them when you're *not* on your period. That way, you won't be all stressed out, thinking, *If I don't get this in during the next 10 seconds, I'm going to be demoted back to my maxi-with-wings!*

Tampons with a plastic applicator are a favorite with many teen girls because they're smoother and seem to slide better than the kind with cardboard. You can also buy tampons with no applicator at all. These are very small and are often good to start with.

Tampon sizes include junior, slender, regular, super, and extra-super absorbent. Once you turn into a tampon pro, you can use different sizes for different parts of your period, saving the extra-super absorbent for those first few days and finishing up with something smaller.

When you get your "collection" together, play with the applicators to see how they operate. Then, starting with a new one you haven't been handling, try inserting one (we'll talk about *how* later). Find the type that works for you, and then get yourself a box for your next period.

But What If? What If? What If?

Before you get started, remember that *most* girls (*very* few exceptions!) have some trouble with tampons the first go-around. This is a whole new gig, so you're bound to be a little clumsy at first . . . probably like the first time you shaved your legs. These are some approaches that can get you off to a good start if you decide to use tampons:

Decide whether you're actually ready. A 15-year-old I talked to—with three years of experience in this menstruation business—advises using the most comfortable pad you can find until you get used to the idea of even having your period. *Then* experiment with tampons if you want. There's no rush!

If you decide this is the day you're going to try tampons, relax. Anxiety actually makes it harder, physically, to get a tampon inserted. When you're nervous, your vaginal muscles tighten involuntarily. Just take a couple of good, deep breaths, and remember you aren't a failure as a woman if it doesn't work the first time!

Know your own body. You've seen pictures of the female reproductive organs in little pamphlets about getting your period, or even in the instructions that come in the tampon box. Take a good look at those, and see how all this works.

Another way is to look at your genitals with a mirror. I didn't actually do that until I was 27 years old and about to have a baby! My doctor set me up with a mirror, and I was fascinated! After all, it's your body—God-made. It's going to take you through a lot in the years to come, so why not get to know it? In this case, it'll show you just where that tampon is supposed to go.

Be willing to experiment. What works for one girl is a failure for another, so play around with positions and types of tampons. If you're going to do this for a week out of every month until you're 50-something, isn't it worth the time to find the best way?

Be patient. When you're young, your vaginal opening is narrow, so it may be a few months, or even a year or two, before your body is ready for tampons. Work *with* your body, not *against* it.

How Do You Get the Thing In? (And Out?)

There's nothing mysterious about putting in a tampon, but try telling that to the girl who's been in the bathroom for 30 minutes, has broken out in a sweat, and has 12 malfunctioned tampons piled up in the trash!

Like anything else, you can start with some simple steps. Nine times out of 10, they'll work for you.

1. Start with the slender or junior size. (Think of it as a tampon with training wheels!)

2. Always wash your hands before inserting or removing a tampon. Then find a comfortable position. Some girls stand with their knees slightly bent. Others put one foot up on the toilet seat, and still others sit on the toilet itself, although most beginners say it's harder when you're sitting down. One "tampon expert" suggests lying on your back on your bed the first time so you can really relax.

3. Take the wrapper off, and hold the tampon in the hand you write with. If you're lying down, raise your knees and spread your legs slightly. Using your other hand, gently part the folds of skin around your vagina. Place the tip of the tampon at your vaginal opening,

and push it inside just a little, maybe 1/4 to 1/2 inch. If you're using a cardboard or plastic applicator, go ahead now and *ease* it in until your fingers touch your skin. Then move the smaller tube, which acts like a plunger to push the tampon into your vagina, into the larger one. Now carefully pull both tubes away, taking care not to pull the tampon out with the applicator. If you're using a tampon with no applicator, push it in as far as you can. You'll be using your finger, so you can feel whether it's in place.

4. Always toss the applicator (whether plastic or cardboard) in the trash can. Flushing them down the toilet spells disaster!

You'll know the tampon is in correctly when:
• you can't feel it when you stand, sit, jump, squat, or lie down.
• the string is hanging free, outside your vaginal opening.
• you can see only the string and no other part of the tampon.

Taking out a tampon is a piece of quiche. Just pull gently on the string, and the whole thing will slide right out. It'll be bigger now because it's absorbed a lot of fluid. Again, even though some tampons are advertised as being flushable, don't chance it. Wrap them up and dispose of them in the trash.

But What If I Can't Get It In?

First of all, if it makes you feel any better, just about everyone who's tried tampons has asked the same question. If you're having tampon troubles, try this trouble-shooting list:

• Maybe your aim is bad. I'm going to tell you a secret I haven't shared with many people before now. I was 21 years old before I figured out how to use a tampon successfully! Really—all through high school and college, every month I'd break out the box and the instructions. Every time, I was an internal-protection drop-out. I'd just about given up when one day I saw a side view of the female body in a diagram, and something caught my eye.

The vagina, I discovered (as everyone else probably had in eighth grade), doesn't go straight up. It kind of angles toward the small of your back. I could barely wait for my next period (if you can believe *that*), and then I aimed that tampon toward my lower back, and bingo—I was on the tampon team.

• Maybe your vagina is really dry. Try putting a water-soluble lubricant like K-Y jelly on the tip of the tampon so it slides in more easily. Just don't use anything with perfume on it, because it can irritate the vagina.

• Perhaps you're pushing the tampon against the skin. With your fingers, separate the folds of skin, and then try it. After a while, you'll just naturally find your way.

• Maybe you're using the wrong size or type for you. If it seems too big, try a slender kind or one of the no-applicator variety. If it won't slide, go for one with a plastic applicator. Ask your mom what she uses. There's nothing like a good discussion about tampons to achieve female bonding!

• Perhaps you need a different position. You don't have to stand on your head, even though your cousin Sarah Jane told you that's the way she does it! There really is no right or wrong way.

• Maybe your body isn't ready. If you have a lot of trouble getting a tampon in and you've tried all of the above, wait a few months and try again. Your vaginal opening will naturally enlarge as you get older.

• If it feels as though something's blocking the way, talk to your mom. You may need to see a doctor—just to check things out. Whether you use tampons or not, some- thing like that would need to be looked at anyway.

What If It's Uncomfortable?

The whole purpose of tampons is to provide a *comfortable* way to get through your period. If it's *uncomfortable*, something's wrong. But don't despair—it can be fixed!

Usually if a tampon hurts or bothers you, it's because it isn't pushed in far enough. Just relax and push it in a little more. If that doesn't work, pull it out and begin again with a fresh one.

The advantage of the no-applicator tampons is that you can usu-ally correct the problem without having to start all over. But whatever you do, don't walk around in pain! Work with it a while and you'll find your own foolproof method. Believe it or not, eventually you won't even think about it. It'll be as easy as opening a bag of potato chips—maybe even easier.

Is It Really Okay to Use Them?

Sometimes the bottom-line question is not "*How* do I use it?" but "*Should* I use it?" There are all kinds of concerns about tampons—and none of them is stupid. It's your body—you need to have your questions answered. These are some of the questions Susie has received through the mail:

Is it okay for a virgin to use tampons? When you use one, does that mean you're not a virgin anymore? A virgin is a person who has never had sexual intercourse. Since that has absolutely *nothing* to do with tampons, you're safe! I think the confusion occurs because there was a time when people thought the breaking of the hymen meant you weren't a virgin, regardless of how it happened.

The hymen is a thin layer of skin that lies across the vaginal opening in some girls at birth. Some girls, by the way, are born without one—but that doesn't mean they aren't virgins when they're 10 minutes old! The hymen has an opening to allow fluid, such as menstrual blood, to pass out of the body, so it's perfectly fine to use a tampon. For a lot of girls, the hymen has already deteriorated naturally by the time they start their periods.

Other girls break it through athletic activities, because any stretching movement can do it. So, whether or not the hymen is still there has *nothing* to do with your sexual status, and it doesn't affect your use of tampons.

Once I have the tampon in, can it get lost inside me? Good question— but not a chance. The only opening between your vagina and the rest of your body is a tiny depression in the center of your cervix called the *Os*. This is the opening through which the menstrual blood leaves the uterus, and it's no bigger than the tip of a match. A tampon absolutely *cannot* go

through it—and there's no other way it could get to another part of your body.

Will it fall out? Not if you have it in right. And you'll know if it isn't in, as we've mentioned above, because you'll be able to feel it. If you can't feel it, it's in there until you take it out by pulling the string. Your vagina is very flexible, and it snuggles in around the tampon to hold it in place. There's also a ring-shaped muscle inside your vagina called the *sphincter*, and it works to hold the tampon in place.

What about toxic shock syndrome (TSS)? TSS is an extremely rare illness that has been associated with the use of superabsorbent tampons. Tampons are not the cause of TSS, because it has also been known to occur in men, children, and non-tampon-using women. Only about 17 out of every 100,000 menstruating women develop TSS each year.

TSS is a bacterial disease, and its connection with tampons is that a normally harmless bacteria in the vagina can multiply out of control and become deadly when a highly absorbent tampon is left in too long.

To lower your risk of getting TSS, use the least-absorbent tampons you can. Don't wait longer than eight hours to change them, even when your period is almost over. Store them in a clean, dry place, and wash your hands with soap and water before inserting or removing a tampon. If during your period you have any symptoms of TSS, remove your tampon right away and see your doctor. Symptoms include: fever, aching muscles, sore throat, nausea, vomiting, headache, big-time diarrhea, and sunburn-like rash or peeling skin from your hands and feet. Basically, if you use tampons the *right* way, you don't have to be worried about TSS.

What If My Mom Says I Can't Use Them?

Moms have the last word, and that last word is to be respected. But there's nothing wrong with sharing new information with your mom. Mothers usually say no because they want to do what's best for you. I have a teenage daughter myself, and I just knew she was going to slit a major artery the first time she shaved her legs or poke an eye out with a mascara wand! But good safety decisions are based on factual information, so show your mother what you've learned here.

You're both women, so you can explore the issue together. Besides, even if you have to wait until you're out on your own to get into the tampon habit, it isn't a tragedy. That'll still give you 30 years to use them!

If you have any more questions—about tampons or anything else you're too embarrassed to ask in health class—consider talking to your mom. I'll bet she'd be thrilled that you decided to come to *her* with the stuff you don't understand![2]

☼ Wrapping It Up ☼

I hope this chapter on the menstrual cycle, cramps, and learning how to insert a tampon has taken you back a few years. It's important for you to remember what it felt like to be unsure of your changing body in order for you to help your daughter cope with hers.

Since God cares about everything that concerns us, let's take this entire subject to Him in prayer—as we will with every topic we cover in this book.

> *Father, I must confess I'd forgotten about all the silly fears and questions I had about my changing body when I was younger. Please help me to take my daughter's concerns seriously. I don't ever want to hear her questions as silly or stupid.*
>
> *Help me to establish a close enough relationship with my daughter that will enable her to come directly to me with questions about her body.*
>
> *Lord, give me wisdom and guidance as she heads into the teen years. I want the next few years to be a smooth transition for her. Show me when to guide, when to push, and when to wait in silence.*
>
> *And thank You, Father, for caring about my daughter's changing body. I love You!*
> *Amen.*

☼ Memorize It . . . with Your Daughter ☼

For you created my inmost being; you knit me together in my mother's womb. I praise you because I am fearfully and wonderfully made; your works are wonderful, I know that full well.

My frame was not hidden from you when I was made in the secret place. When I was woven together in the depths of the earth, your eyes saw my unformed body. (Psalm 139:13–16)

Give Your Daughter the Right Heroes
Is Your Daughter in Love with N Snyc? Don't Panic!

Sheree's bedroom is plastered with posters of the Indigo Girls, the Backstreet Boys, and countless other musicians and actors who are the media's current hot items. Though she's an active member of her church's youth group and Bible study, she's also immersed in *Entertainment Tonight's* scoop on who's who and who's doing what.

"Should we be concerned?" her mom asks Sheree's father.

"A lot of girls her age have teen idols," he responds.

"I guess that's true. I just wish we could somehow influence whom she idolizes."

Good News

Guess what? As parents, you *can* influence—to a degree—who your daughter's heroes are! While it's normal for our teens to admire current celebrities in the world, our responsibility as parents is to provide them with biblical alternatives. That only makes sense, doesn't it? If we care enough to provide them with contemporary Christian music as an alternative to secular rock, godly standards in lieu of the world's permissiveness, and family entertainment over R-rated options, why wouldn't we care enough to give our daughters biblical and inspirational heroes instead of rock stars?

We Do Care!

It's my guess that's what we'd *like* to do, but we just aren't sure how. One of the reasons we could be floundering may be simply that we draw a blank when trying to come up with solid options. Here are my suggestions:

Educating Yourself

Give your mind and heart a refresher course on biblical heroes. Here's a quick rundown of a few who stand out in *my* mind:

- *Ruth*—She was willing to leave her homeland and security to follow her mother-in-law and maintain a godly lifestyle. She trusted God to meet her needs for food, shelter, and even a husband. I'd say that's pretty relevant! Transition that to your daughter's fears or insecurities about friends and relationships.

- *Abraham*—He left his home for a place he couldn't even *see!* He may not even have been sure it *existed*—yet he trusted the Lord's guidance and wisdom. The result? God blessed him more than he could ever have imagined. Transition: Dare to dream big! Abraham asked for one son, yet God gave him descendants who eventually outnumbered even the stars in the sky. God cares about what's important to you. He dreams big for you!

- *Daniel*—He went against popular culture determined to maintain an intimate, growing relationship with God.

Transition: Everyone else may not seem to be affected by hearing God's name in vain, cheating on their homework, or what the latest Top-10 radio hit suggests, but not everyone else is interested in living a godly life. Our heavenly Father is calling us to raise the standard—even if it means standing alone. Daniel prayed three times a day while others mocked him. Compare that to standing alone at the school flagpole on "See You at the Pole" day or bowing your head and giving thanks for your meal in the school cafeteria. It's not easy to take a stand—but it's right.

Educating Your Daughter

After you have some heroes in mind, talk with your daughter about them. Make creative transitions from "those days" to "these days" as suggested above. Help her see the relevance that biblical heroes can offer.

Finding Heroes outside the Bible

There are also plenty of godly role models throughout history who are worth noting. Does your church have a list of missionaries who have been instrumental in spreading the gospel in other parts of the world? If so, acquaint your daughter with these biographies. What about Jim Elliot, who was killed in Ecuador by the Auca Indians? And his wife (who's still alive), Elisabeth Elliot, who later ministered to those same Indians and even baptized their grandchildren. Are these names familiar to your daughter? What about missionary Hudson Taylor? Introduce her to his hardships and adventures on the mission field.

Corrie Ten Boom and Mother Teresa are other good examples. Corrie's story teaches us an incredible amount about perseverance, forgiveness, and emotional healing. Mother Teresa's various ministries from orphanages to leper colonies inspire us to get outside our comfort zones and be "Jesus" to those around us.

Finding Heroes Who Are Active and Making a Difference Today

In a day when being in the spotlight seems to be everything, contemporary Christian artist Rebecca St. James offers a refreshing humility. I had the privilege of traveling with Rebecca and her family for almost a month for her annual Christmas tour. It wasn't uncommon to see her scrubbing the floor of the motor home, bagging up trash, and helping others with their luggage. Instead of demanding star status, she's intensely focused on maintaining a servant's heart.

> ☼
>
> *"I love it when my mom and I get to do stuff together —even if it's just watching television or making a sandwich. I love being with her."*
> Kelly, fifteen

Know what Rebecca did in the fall of 1999? She took two months off from singing and paid her own way to Romania to serve in an orphanage. No singing. No stage. No star status— just simple servanthood.

I spent some time with her in Romania and again was impressed by her humility. She was just as content holding babies, doing laundry, and working her fingers to the bone as she was in front of a crowd and singing behind a microphone.

Rebecca also speaks openly about sexual purity, family closeness, and disciplined spiritual growth. Hmmm. Sounds like a modern-day hero for *any* teen girl!

How can you find other modern-day godly role models? Provide your daughter with Christian literature that's often filled with current examples. We regularly highlight female role models in *Brio* magazine. You may also want to check out *Guideposts, Christianity Today,* or *Today's Christian Woman.*

Her Bedroom Walls

Your daughter may still want to hang a poster of N Snyc in her room, and if so, don't panic. The key is to teach your daughter how to discern. *Every* celebrity isn't really a star. But as *Christians,* we can *all* shine like stars to a lost and hope-seeking world. (Memorize Philippians 2:15–16 together.)

Preteen to Teen: Making the Transition Easier

Dear Diary:

Mom just doesn't get it! Why can't she see that I'm a teenager? Well . . . practically a teen. Okay, even though I'm still eleven, I'm already in the teen world. Why can't she see that? She treats me like such a baby.

"Where are you going, Aubrey?"

"HAVE YOU CLEANED YOUR ROOM, AUBREY?"

"AUBREY, DON'T FORGET TO TAKE YOUR VITAMINS."

Gimme a break! I'm not a little kid anymore!

Ugh!

Tomorrow's Friday, and Chelsey and I get to spend the night together. Her dad's taking us to Sesame Street Live! Can't wait. We've got seats on the third row. I luuuv it when they walk right to the edge of the stage!

Gotta go! My brother, Jeremy, and I are collecting aluminum cans to see how much money we can get.

Hey Diary:

Today was awful. School was the pits. I forgot our book reports were due today, and I didn't have mine. At lunch I spilled milk on my pants. Lindsey and Danielle kept making fun of me all day and told everyone I wet my pants. Even Aaron was laughing at me.

THEN DURING AFTERNOON BREAK, I TRIPPED AND RIPPED THE HEM OUTTA MY PANTS. MARK CALLED ME A KLUTZ. MRS. JOHNSON GAVE ME DETENTION FOR BEING TARDY, AND I TOTALLY HATE MY LIFE!

I'm getting a zit on my nose—I can feel it coming in—and it hurts as bad as childbirth—I just know it! I didn't get home in time to help Jeremy take all our aluminum cans to the recycler, and I know he's gonna keep all the money.

I wish Mom would hurry up and get home. I can't wait for her to sit on the couch and go through the mail so I can crawl in her lap and cry on her shoulder.

HURRRRRRRY, MOM!!!!!!!!

Diary Dearest:

You're the only one who understands. Nobody else gets me. They all act like I'm two years old or something. Sheesh!

I ask for so little. And I get nothing. Nada. ZILCH. ZIPPO.

All I wanted to do was go to the mall to meet Nathan and Brent. No big deal, right? It's only two miles from here! I'm not even asking for a ride. I was gonna take my bike.

But, no!

"It's too far for you to ride alone."

"You shouldn't be just hanging out at the mall with two boys."

"Something could happen."

Like what?!! I'm thinking. I'm gonna spend a bunch of money or something? I don't even own any money! I couldn't even call home from a pay phone at the mall! What are they thinking???

Gotta go. Almost time for *Family Matters* reruns.

Di:
   I'm sooooo jazzed. Mom's gonna let me ride the bus home with Allison so we can play with our new Beanie Babies! Can't wait. She's got like a trazillion-gillion!
   Later.

A Little Girl or a Young Lady?

Every preteen girl and every mother in America face the battle of a little girl wanting to grow up too fast. As you read Aubrey's journal entries, you probably noticed that she wants to do adult things yet quickly vacillates back to her childhood comfort zone. The same is probably true of your preteen daughter. In the morning, she wants her independence, by noon she's back to dolls or Beanie Babies, by evening she's wanting freedom to hang with friends away from adult supervision, but by nighttime she's yearning to cuddle and crawls into your lap.

What's going on? Is she a little girl, or is she a young lady? Well, let's just say that she's *normal*. And part of being normal is being caught right in the middle of a tough transition from little girl to young lady.

If you're confused by her behavior, take heart—she's even more confused than you are! Helping her in a smooth journey from one phase of life to the next is every mom's dream. But when she goes back and forth so fast, how can you predict what's next? And what battles are you in for during the next couple of years?

Let's take a look at some of the most popular issues preteen girls and their moms deal with during this frustrating time.

Makeup Madness

Since your daughter is inundated with a push from magazines, movies, and television to look beautiful, it's only a matter of time before she begins asking about makeup.

There's really no reason she needs to begin wearing much more than lip gloss before she turns thirteen. And when she *does* reach that magical teenage birthday, create your first makeup-buying date, an event she'll never forget!

Make an appointment for her at one of the cosmetic counters at a reputable store in the mall. Let a professional apply her makeup and explain what she's doing and why. This will teach your daughter the correct way to apply her makeup, and it will also prevent her from getting the "too-gooped-up" look.

You know what else it'll teach her? She'll realize that you care about the things that concern *her* during these upcoming teen years. And that's exactly what you want, Mom! You *want* your daughter to know that if it's important to her, it's important to you.

Smooth Shaving

Your ten-year-old daughter wants to start shaving her legs. "Jenna's mom lets her," she says. "And Adriene and Janelle are doing it too." How will you react?

"I wish my mom wouldn't get so bent out of shape when I forget to put a new roll of toilet paper on!"

Tara, thirteen

Is your daughter physically coordinated enough to handle shaving her legs? I don't think age has as much to do with this one as matutity does. For instance, there ate some ten-year-old girls whoare more mature than fifteen-year-olds.

Mom, this one is totally your call. But here's what I think: If there's a good enough reason for her to begin shaving this early, and if she's adept enough at handling a razor so that she won't cut a pint-sized hole in her leg, consider letting her do it.

What kind of reasons are good enough? Perhaps she's wearing

more dresses than pants or jeans and her friends are making fun of her for having hairy legs. If most of her friends are shaving their legs, she'll want to begin shaving hers. Or maybe she has dark hair and she's becoming self-conscious about her legs. Again, anything you can do to build positive self-esteem in your daughter is to your benefit.

This just doesn't seem like an important battle to fight. And there *will* be plenty of other battles worth saving your energy for later! Choose your battles carefully, moms. If it's really *not* a big deal, don't make it one.

Getting with Guys

Your daughter is beginning to show an interest in guys. *She* says she's ready to date. *You* know she's not. How do you handle this battle?

First of all, ask her to explain to you what a date is. Who knows? In her mind, it may simply be sitting next to a guy in church. Then again, it may mean getting into the car of a seventeen-year-old and being gone the entire evening.

At any rate, it's important that you find out exactly what she's thinking. To make sure you're both on the same page, get her definition of dating and give her yours. Together, come to a mutual decision as to what dating *is*, so you can create a plan of action as to when it's acceptable to actually begin dating.

For preteens between fifth grade and ninth grade, "going out" doesn't really mean *going* anywhere! After all, no one can even drive yet! It usually means "we're together," which is defined as sitting together, eating lunch together at school, walking through the hallways together, and being together at after-hours school activities (athletic games, club meetings, etc.).

These preteen years are a fantastic time to help your daughter begin to understand the opposite sex and learn to be comfortable around guys . . . as *friends!* Many Christian parents simply tell their daughters, "No dating until you're sixteen." Can you use this rule for your own daughter? Maybe. Maybe not. You probably know your daughter better than anyone; therefore, you're the best judge of her maturity factor. Just like knowing when to let her begin shaving her legs, this is a call only you can make.

I *hope* you won't allow your daughter to begin dating before she's sixteen years old, but when your preteen is begging to simply "do stuff" with guys, what's your answer? That's not really dating . . . yet do you want her establishing relationships with guys before she's actually a teenager?

Again, I believe these years can best be spent teaching your daughter how to become good *friends* with guys—as well as girls. These are the years when she's shaping and changing her personality. She's learning how to start a conversation and how to ask thinking questions that keep a discussion going. In short, she's at the stage of learning what's socially acceptable and what's not.

If your daughter is putting pressure on you to allow her to spend time with guys, I advise:

Only in a group of guys and girls—and you need to know the guys in the group. Perhaps a circle of friends from church is wanting to eat pizza while you're involved in a parent meeting with the youth pastor.

Only in a controlled setting that you have approved. Your daughter is invited to a video party on Friday evening at the house of some of your friends from church. You not only know the kids who will be there, you're good friends with the parents, and you know your daughter won't be allowed to leave the house or be unchaperoned.

Only in an environment in which you are present. If your daughter won't let up on hanging out with guys, suggest that she invite guys *and* girls over to your house for a pizza-making party. Again . . . guys and girls whom you know and are comfortable with.

Not at all. There's absolutely nothing wrong with you simply saying, "No. You're not ready for guy/girl situations yet."

Picky. Picky. Picky.

Why am I being so conservative about a preteen girl hanging out with guys? Because the sooner she becomes comfortable being in a social situation with guys, the faster she'll expect to continue to experience social situations with guys.

But wait a minute, Susie! You just stated a few minutes ago that these are great years to help my daughter become comfortable in social situations with guys.

You're right, I did. And I'm all for teaching our young daughters how to communicate effectively with the opposite sex—becoming good conversationalists and learning appropriate social skills—but I *don't* feel good about our preteens becoming so comfortable around the opposite sex that they tend to "expect" to get to do things with guys. Our preteen daughters are growing up fast as it is; when they're invited to a party or an activity where guys will be present, it should feel like a special occasion—not the norm.

Caution: Look at this section as a flashing yellow light! It's important for you to remember that most ten-year-old girls aren't interested in the opposite sex. And though your eleven- or twelve-year-old daughter may begin to show signs of becoming interested, please remember that guys her age are *not* interested in her! Since girls mature at a faster pace than guys, the eleven-year-old males she knows still think she has "cooties" and are much more interested in worms, dirt, and grossing out their friends than they are in your daughter.

So if your eleven- or twelve-year-old preteen daughter is expressing an interest in the opposite sex, she's looking at older guys. Your twelve-year-old daughter may be an early bloomer *physically*, but *emotionally* she's still only twelve years old! You may think it's time for you to intervene when a fifteen- or sixteen-year-old boy starts paying attention to your twelve-year-old, but guess what? The time to intervene is waaaay before that! Start setting boundaries right *now* so your daughter knows she can't even entertain the possibility of hanging out with teen guys!

Too Much, Too Fast

A few months ago, I flew from Sydney, Australia, to San Francisco. I was not looking forward to the fourteen-hour flight, and I really wanted to simply close my eyes and pretend I didn't exist for the next day in the air.

But before takeoff, the airline attendant approached the empty seat next to me with a fourteen-year-old girl. "The row she was assigned to is really cramped," the flight attendant explained. "And since you're on the exit row with extra leg room and an empty seat, I'd like to move her next to the window."

So Tonya settled into 22A and began sorting through her necessities—you know, the stuff she'd need for the next fourteen hours: her portable CD player, collection of fifty-two CDs, makeup kit, stationery and friends' addresses, stuffed bear, slippers, and chocolate.

After she had stored the rest of her bags, she buckled her seat belt and looked at me. "Hi," I mumbled, disappointed that I wouldn't be able to stretch across the seats.

"Hey!" she said . . . a little loudly. "Aren't you the lady who does *Brio* magazine? Huh? Are you Susie?"

"Yes, I am. Do you get *Brio?*"

"Yeah! Cool. This is great—we can talk!"

Even though the airline showed four movies, served three meals, offered us drinks at five different times, and provided music and magazines for us, Tonya was pretty much interested in only one thing—talking!

For the next several hours this fourteen-year-old (who *looked* like a sixteen-year-old) went on and on about how her mother just didn't have a clue when it came to Tonya's life.

"She just doesn't get it!" Tonya explained. "I wanna hang out with guys, you know? And they wanna hang out with me. But my mom won't let me date yet. Hello. I'm not asking to *date* date, I just wanna be *with* guys—you know, go to the movies, hang out at the mall, you know . . . like *be* with them."

"Tonya," I began, "why do you think your mom is saying you can't do that?"

"Oh, she keeps saying something could happen. I'm so sure!"

"Well . . . *could* something happen?"

"I don't know. Maybe."

"How old are the guys you're wanting to hang with?" I pressed.

"They're all older than me. Most of them are like sixteen or seventeen. They've got cars."

"So what are you going to do? Obey your mom and wait till you're older, or what?"

"Nah. I'm already hanging out with these guys—she just doesn't know it. I mean, like, I can't really help it. It's not like I'm disobeying her or anything. But I'll, you know, be at the mall, and older guys will just come up to me and start hanging out with me. A few times they've even made passes at me—you know, tried to get physical with me and stuff. It's kinda scary!"

What's wrong with this picture? A beautiful fourteen-year-old girl who is physically endowed to look like a sixteen- or seventeen-year-old is naturally going to attract older guys. Her mom was wise in not allowing her daughter to hang out with them, but her mom was blowing it by giving Tonya too much freedom too soon. Should Tonya have even been hanging out at the mall with-out an adult? That's where she was meeting up with older guys.

By the end of the flight, I was grateful I'd had a chance to sit next to and talk with Tonya. I was able to affirm her yet at the same time encourage her to slow down and stick with kids her own age.

Did it make a difference in her life? Probably not. But maybe some seeds were planted.

Is that yellow caution light still blinking? Don't let your daughter grow up too fast, Mom! And don't give her too much freedom too fast. Again, she may *look* like she's ready to handle some extra responsibility; but remember, she's still a little girl.

Buying a Bra

Some of your daughter's friends are wearing bras. Your daugh-ter is expressing interest in one too. Is she ready for one? Does she need one? Maybe she simply wants to be like her friends. Should you let her get a bra?

My advice is: If she needs one (as soon as you can see that she's developing), don't wait until she asks you about it. Make it a spe-cial event! *You* approach *her* and take her shopping. Chances are, if you wait until she mentions it, she's already feeling self-conscious. Come on, moms! Take the initiative and beat her to it!

Even if she's not quite ready for one but wants one, what's the harm in letting her have one? It won't hurt her to wear a bra, and as her mom, anything you can do to build her self-confidence is a positive thing.

But since it's been a few years since you've purchased your first bra, let's review what's important in shopping for a bra. You'll want to go *with* your daughter the first time, but she *will* reach a point where she'll want to do her own shopping for undergarments. And when she's ready to shop alone, you can pass along this great lesson on finding the right fit. (Read it first yourself, though, so you'll be reminded of what's important when helping her purchase her first bra.)

Complete Guide to Buying a Bra

By Kathryn Springer

Okay, so shopping for undergarments isn't as much fun as renting a video and munching on popcorn. But, hey, it doesn't have to be weird, either.

The store is crowded. You wander past the perfume counter and stop to try some of the testers. Suddenly, a perfectly made-up clerk approaches. You smile and run—leaving a scent of vanilla-sunflower-musk trailing behind.

Darting past jewelry and other accessories, you slow down and pretend to admire a group of purses as several people walk by. Your next stalling tactic is to take your time in the shoe department. (Uh . . . maybe a pair of clogs?)

Then you see it—just ahead of you. A maze of spandex and satin and flowered cotton. The lingerie department. *Gulp.* Looks quiet. A quick scan of the area shows there's no one lurking behind the underwear bins. Why does the lingerie department have to be bordered by the aisle that looks like a superhighway? Do they *plan* it that way?

Here goes. You duck into the maze and your vision blurs. How in the world are you supposed to sort through all this? Cotton. Satin. Sports bras. Underwires. And the sizes! Large. Larger-than-life. And the "Am-I-ever-going-to-develop?" size.

You take a deep breath and suddenly. . . .

"Can I help you?"

You freeze and break into a sweat at the same time. *The lingerie lady!*

"Do you need help finding a bra?"

The store must use this woman instead of a speaker system.

Uh . . . what do you say?

Game Plan

Shopping for a bra doesn't *have* to be a totallyembarrassing, totallyuncool, painful experience. Approach it the same way you would if you were buying a pair of shoes. Know your size (or have a good idea), and think about what you like and about your lifestyle. Although you may think that a bra isn't an important part of your wardrobe because it doesn't "show," a well-fitting bra will actually help your clothes look better.

Believe it or not, at one time when women shopped for a bra, they were measured right there in the store by the lingerie lady. *Yikes!* What if she measures you, clucks her tongue, smiles, and says, "Not yet, dear"? Although there *is* greater accuracy if someone *else* does the measuring, you can still do it yourself and get pretty close results. Here's how:

• Find a tape measure (check Mom's sewing kit, *not* Dad's tool box!). Don't pull the tape measure tightly around yourself, but *do* keep it snug.

• To determine your *bra* size, measure around the chest, just under your arms and above your bust. Measurements that include a fraction should be rounded up. You can double-check your bra size by measuring around your ribs—just below your bust—and adding five inches. Say you measure 31 inches around your ribs, then your bra size would be 36. If your measurement is 33 inches or more, add only three inches instead of five. And, if it turns out that your bra size is an odd number, round up to the next even number since bras come in even sizes: 32, 34, 36, etc.

• To find your *cup* size, measure around the fullest part of your bust, again not pulling the tape tight. The difference between the measurements (your bra size measurement taken earlier and the bust measurement you just took) equals the cup size. For example, if there is no difference, the cup size is AA. If there is a one-inch difference, the cup size is A. For a two-inch difference the size is B, and a three-inch difference would be C.

You Can Do It!

Now that you have a good idea

of what size you're looking for, you can take that information into the lingerie department armed with confidence. (No more guessing, grabbing a stash of bras and darting into the nearest dressing room!)

A bra that fits well shouldn't feel tight or leave marks on your skin. But the straps shouldn't end up down around your elbows, either! A well-fitting bra will lay flat between your breasts. There shouldn't be any gaps between your skin and the center of the bra.

Although you could probably treat six friends to hot fudge sundaes for the price of some of the bras you'll find, consider them a worthwhile investment. Don't settle for "cheap" just because of the "no-show" factor.

And what about those six friends? Should they come with you? Hmmm. Depends. Maybe you want some moral support but don't really want anyone in the dressing room with you. That's okay. Your mom, an older sister, or a close friend makes a great "lookout," too!

So Many Choices

When you enter the lingerie maze, have an idea of what you want. Bras are generally displayed in groups by brand name; so you'll likely find a mixture of types in the same area.

Sports bras are popular, although some salespeople will tell you they shouldn't be worn every day. They're designed to compress the bust in order to reduce movement during activities such as jogging, basketball, or aerobic exercise. If you like the smooth look of a sports bra, there are seamless bras made with similar fabric that don't compress.

Underwire bras are designed for added support.

Convertible bras have movable straps that are designed to hide under difficult dresses, like those with keyhole backs or off-the-shoulder styles (like the dress you wore for your cousin's wedding or last year's homecoming event).

You Go, Girl!

Consider wearing your favorite shirt when you go shopping for a bra. Don't just try on the bra; put your shirt on over it. Do you like the way it looks? Maybe the straps show. You may want to pick one that has a narrower strap. Does it look *and* feel good?

There are many styles and fabrics available, and you may need to try on several to decide which one you like the best. Flesh-colored bras blend with skin tone and are less likely to show under sheer fabrics.

If the "lingerie lady" approaches (and she probably will), just give her a friendly smile and tell the truth. If you need assistance, simply say, "I'm looking for the sports bras. Can you show me where they are?" Or, if you'd rather be alone and browse, she'll respect that, too. "I'm just looking now, but I'll let you know if I need help" is enough.

Growing physically doesn't happen by itself; it's usually accompanied by emotional growth as well. Having to face challenging, embarrassing, and even uncomfortable situations is part of life. If you still need psyching up, close your eyes and pretend the bra you're holding in your hand is a pair of brand-new Nikes![1]

Phone Problems

Your daughter probably discovered the telephone when she was four or five, but now it seems like it's permanently attached to her. You've noticed that she's been talking to her girlfriends quite a bit on the phone during the past year, but recently you've overheard her talking with boys. How will you react?

Let's do some investigating first, okay? Approach her non-chalantly and find out if she's calling the boys or if the boys are calling her. Next, find out who the boys are. Perhaps she's talking to her cousin or a childhood friend from church with whom she's sung in choir or gone to amusement parks and family get-togethers.

Before you decide what's acceptable and what's not, let's look at both sides. I used to work with a woman who had some strict rules concerning her daughter's use of the phone. "Krystal isn't allowed to call guys—ever," Cindy told me. "Her dad and I feel strongly about this. If a boy wants to talk with her, he can take the initiative. We don't want her chasing guys."

As far as they knew, Krystal followed the rules—for the time being. But when she turned eighteen, this young lady, who was involved heavily in her youth group and bringing friends to church and seemingly fired-up for God, did a ninety-degree turn. She not only moved out of the house, she told her parents that she was sick and tired of their "stupid rules" and wouldn't put up with them any longer.

Her parents were dumbfounded . . . and heartbroken.

Connie, on the other hand, took a different approach with her teen daughter. "My husband and I decided that we didn't want to make it a big deal. She *does* call guys when she's arranging a ride to a youth group activity or organizing a party with teens from church. Most of the time, though, she's talking to girls on the phone."

"Yeah, but what if she *did* start calling guys . . . you know, just to chat?" I asked.

"It would depend on the guys she called. Most of the guys she's friends with, though, are guys from our church youth group. Guys she's grown up with. We know these boys, and we know their families."

"What if guys start calling her more . . . you know, just to chat?" I continued.

"Again, we don't want to call attention to it, because as soon as we do, it becomes an issue. Right now she looks at these guys the same way she does her girlfriends—as good friends."

If the situation got out of hand, of course, Connie and her husband would intervene, but they're allowing Marie some freedom to make her own decisions—on a limited basis—with the phone.

It seems there should always be room for compromise—especially in areas that don't need to become big battles. I see the phone as falling into this category. Krystal's parents made it such a big deal that it finally *became* an issue—as did several other things.

But chances are that Marie will never see the phone as an issue, because her parents haven't made it a battle worth fighting.

Um . . . Uh . . . Well . . .

Since this is the time when your daughter is learning social skills and how to carry on a conversation, you may want to give her some telephone hints. Many girls are so surprised even to *get* a call from a guy that they become speechless. Not good.

Here's a fun reminder of what it can be like to be nervous on the phone and how to turn that nervousness into a balanced conversation. (Show this to your daughter, okay?)

AT&T and Me

Okay, so you've been waiting by the phone for almost a whole hour hoping, *wishing*, PRAYING he'll call. He finally does, and when you pick up the receiver you're so nervous you answer the phone by screaming, "IT'S ABOUT TIME, YOU GORGEOUS SLOW POKE!"

Wrong move. If he doesn't hang up immediately, he'll tell all the guys at school the next day *never* to call you. *Hmmm.* Guess this means it's time for a few lessons on phone etiquette. *Sound boring?* Okay, we'll go with "How to keep him hanging on instead of hanging up."

What to Do When He Calls You

Be excited!

Believe it or not, girls, it's scary for a guy to call you! A trillion things are zooming around in his head. Stuff like:

- *Is she gonna think I'm in love with her just because I called?*

- *What if she doesn't want to talk to me?*

- *If I say something stupid is she gonna spread it all over school tomorrow?*

- *What if I forget what I'm gonna say and just sit there like a dweeb?*

Pretty scary thoughts, huh? Guess what? We girls have the power to make or break a phone conversation. That's right. Once a guy *does* call us, we can help make him feel glad he did. How?

By being excited.

When a guy knows you're excited he called, he immediately feels more comfortable talking to you. Chances are he'll probably even call you again!

Warning: Don't overdo it. Remember, he's already scared. Coming on too strong may make him back off.

Bad response: "Wow! Is it really you? Like totally awesome! I can't believe you called. Too cool. Have you called any other girls today or am I the first one? I can't wait to tell Jennifer. Everyone said you were too chicken to pick up the phone! Like wow! I'm so excited."

Good response: "Hi, Chad! It's good to hear from you!"

Help Him Out with the Conversation

Since you know it's a big deal for him to call in the first place, don't make him do all the work. Show him you're glad he called by doing your part to keep the conversation going. Ask him questions about things he's interested in. Talk about your church youth group activities, school functions, or anything you have in common.

Bad response: "Aren't you gonna say anything?"

Good response: "I think I'll do my book report on a fun book called *Getting Ready for the Guy/Girl Thing.* What are you going to do yours on?"

Answer Questions with More Than Just Yes and No

If you're simply giving quick, short answers to the questions he's asking, he'll get frustrated and hang up. Why? Because you're making him carry the weight of the conversation. Too much pressure for a guy who's already nervous.

When you answer a question, explain your answer. Don't go overboard and give him an oral essay over the phone, but keep the conversation alive by answering in complete sentences.

He asks, "Are you going to the pep rally tomorrow after school?"

Bad response: "No." He needs to hear more, or he'll start thinking stuff like: *She's not going because she knows I'm going to be there. I should've never called!*

> *"I'd love it if my mom were more supportive! I wish she'd tell me that she believed in me."*
>
> Celeste, seventeen

Good response: "No. I really hate it that I can't go, but I have a dentist appointment. Are you going?" If he is, ask him to tell you all about it later. This assures you of getting another phone call from him. (Tee hee. We're pretty sneaky, aren't we, girls?)

He asks, "Are you trying out for cheerleader this year?"

Bad response: "No, and I can't believe you even asked me

that question! You know I get dizzy doing cartwheels. It all started with that car wreck during last summer's family vacation. We were driving through Yellowstone National Park and a bear stepped out on the road in front of us. My dad swerved to miss the bear and our car turned over. I received multiple bruises, three scars, and a concussion. I've been dizzy ever since."

Remember, he doesn't want an oral essay over the phone. Just give him a good, polite sentence.

Good response: "No, I don't think so. Since I joined the band I've been pretty busy with extra rehearsals. But from all the girls I've heard are trying out, I think we'll have a good squad, don't you?"

End with Hope

You can make sure he'll call you again or see you, by giving him *specific* hope. Point him to the future (as in tomorrow, not the distant future). This makes him glad that he called and gives him confidence. (Isn't it neat that you can make a guy feel confident when he's around you?) Wait until the end of the phone call to use this.

Bad response: "Well, maybe I'll see you around."

Good response: "I'll see you tomorrow at school, okay?" (You've given him a *specific* place to look for you, and by phrasing it as a question, you give him an opportunity to agree with you before he hangs up. This will not only help him *remember* to look for you at school tomorrow, but will help him *want* to see you at school tomorrow. Why? Because he knows *you* want to see *him*.)

But if he *doesn't* swing by your locker? If he *doesn't* look for you? That's totally okay. Don't go looking for *him!* As a female, you want to be pursued. Don't be the pursuer!

Always Thank Him for Calling

Remember . . . it was a big deal for him to pick up the phone. And the exciting part is that out of all the girls he *could* have called, he chose to call *you!* That's great. So let him know you appreciate it (without getting too mushy, of course). Again, this makes him feel good about his phone call. It will also make him want to call you again.

Bad response: "Well, uh . . . bye."

Good response: "Thanks for calling, Tony. Bye."

Bad response: "I still can't believe you called *me!* Thanks sooo much. I hope I can get to sleep tonight. Please call me again. Tell me when you're going to call next and I'll sit right here by the phone and wait, okay? Ryan? Hello?"

Good response: "Ryan, thanks for calling. It was fun talking with you. Bye."[2]

But There Are Boundaries

Obviously, if your daughter is on the phone several hours a day with guys, and if she's flirting or dropping hints that she likes them or making plans to "get together," you need to intervene. Outside of simple friendship—which would include organizing parties, rides, activities for youth group, etc.—why would your daughter *need* to call guys?

> "Mom . . . just let me be upset sometimes!"
>
> Kayla, fifteen

I have three good-looking nephews. My brother and his wife are amazed at how many calls from girls they receive. Sometimes they're tempted to say, "If he wants to talk with you, he can call you himself."

When the girl is doing all the calling, it's time to intervene.

I'm friends with a couple at church who have a teen boy. Josh is athletic, involved in church, and just a top-notch guy. He'd be a great catch for any girl! And I guess the girls know it, because his phone is constantly ringing. I was having dinner with the family one night when David answered the phone. I really liked what I heard him say: "I'm sorry, but Josh's mom and I don't allow him to accept calls from girls. You'll probably see him at school tomorrow."

Whether Josh realizes it or not (and by the way, he's so into basketball, he doesn't really have time for girls right now), his dad is paving the way for Josh to be the pursuer instead of being pursued. Though girls will still chase him at school, Josh is learning an important lesson: It's *his* role to be the initiator.

Maybe you've noticed a real lack of leadership among teen guys and young men today. Could part of the reason be that during the past eight or nine years girls have become more aggressive? It's gotten to where guys don't *have* to take the initiative anymore; several girls will be glad to do it for them! That's a sad reflection on our teen girls as well as their parents.

Moms, please work really hard to instill selfconfidence in your daughter. When I see a girl going after guy after guy after guy, the first thing I notice is a lack of self-esteem. The next thing I notice is an unhealthy or nonexistent relationship with her father. Let's teach our daughters to be pursued. After all, your girl *is* worth the wait!

☼ Wrapping It Up ☼

Moms, your daughter is a valuable princess. What are you doing, specifically, to help her see herself this way? She's a unique creation of the King of kings. Teach her how cherished and priceless she is.

Father, I need Your continued guidance during these preteen years. I want to choose my battles carefully. Show me what's worth fighting for and what simply needs discussing.

Lord, I also want to be flexible. Teach me how to bend when I need to bend and how to stand firm when I need to stand. Father, I want my daughter to be socially skilled at making friends and carrying on a conversation. It's been so long since I had to worry about what to say to someone I cared about. Help me to keep focused on my daughter's needs and concerns.

I want to teach her that she doesn't need to be the pursuer, because she's definitely worth the wait! Jesus, help me to make time to pray with her this week.

Amen.

☼ *Memorize It . . . with Your Daughter* ☼

Finally, brothers, whatever is true, whatever is noble, whatever is right, whatever is pure, whatever is lovely, whatever is admirable—if anything is excellent or praiseworthy—think about such things. (Philippians 4:8)

Is Your Home a Safe Haven?
Creating a Positive Environment for Your Daughter Also Helps Create Self-Confidence

Your daughter, Mandi, is having a tough day. She failed her math test—the one she studied two hours for! But instead of coming home after school, she stops by Allison's house and shares her frustration.

Last week, Mandi was having trouble with a group of older girls who picked on her during lunchtime. She cried on Sheila's shoulder.

And yesterday, when Josh found out Mandi liked him, he told his friend Zack to tell *her* that he'd rather be dead than get caught with Mandi! She drowned her sorrow in a big cookie and a little carton of milk at the mall with Kristen.

Though you're grateful she has some good friends in whom to confide, you secretly wish she were coming home with her problems. Hmmm. Maybe it's time to check your home's foundation.

What's Your Home Like?

If your daughter is seeking refuge in other homes, let's take a few seconds to consider the following:

- Does your daughter feel good about being home?
- Does she feel safe in your home?
- Does she feel loved in your home?
- Does your house feel like a home?
- Does your daughter feel she can totally be herself at home?

Reconstructing Your Home

I'll bet one of your goals as a parent is to provide your daughter with a safe place to be nurtured and to grow. Perhaps there are some positive changes you can implement to create this kind of home environment. Let's brainstorm a few, okay?

What if you committed to interest? Actively show interest in your daughter's life. Never give her a reason to tell a friend, "My parents don't care." Make sure she knows you do.

Often parents are tempted to combat this argument with, "Well, I don't show much interest in her life because she never shows any interest in mine!"

Okay. Take a deep breath. Can I be blunt? Be a parent! Your teen isn't interested in what you did at work today. So what? She's a teenager! Memorize Philippians 2:4: "Don't just think about your own affairs, but be interested in others, too, and in what they are doing" (TLB).

Get excited about what *she's* excited about. Whether it's joining the Beanie Babies collectors club or scouting out garage sales on Saturday mornings, take an interest in what she likes.

What if you committed to optimism? If you want your home to be a positive environment, make a choice to keep a positive attitude! We often use God as a crutch here. "Well, I hope God will help me be more positive." Or, "I'm praying for a better attitude."

That's great, but so much of life comes down to simple choices. Do you realize you can maintain spiritual joy in the midst of defeat? You can exhibit peace even when you're searching for answers. You can be positive when you've had a bad day. How would your home environment change if you made those choices? Would your daughter feel better about being home?

Teens enjoy being in a positive place with a happy atmosphere. So much of their everyday lives is spent dealing with changes, stress, shifting values, and peer pressure. When a teen comes *home*, I hope your home can be a positive difference from the world.

Memorize Philippians 4:4 for the motivation to choose a positive attitude and produce a positive environment: "Always be full of joy in the Lord; I say it again, rejoice!" (TLB).

What if you committed to creating a peaceful home? I believe God wants Christian homes to be a place of rest for our chil-

"I wish my mom and I could talk more."

Nikki, fourteen

dren. Think about it: Your daughter is in battle all day long. She needs a place of rest at the end of the day. When others are criticizing, when she finds out she failed the math quiz, or when Josh won't look at her, she needs a haven. Your home can be the shelter from all her storms. She—along with every teen in her zip code —desperately needs that!

Check out Proverbs 14:26: "Reverence for God gives a man deep strength; his children have a place of refuge and security" (TLB).

Hmmm. Guess whose responsibility it is to create such a peaceful environment? Yours. But don't worry. You're not alone. Your heavenly Father will equip you with everything you need to create a safe, godly, positive atmosphere. But it starts with you. It's a matter of choice. Make your decision. *Now.*

Eating Disorders:
They Can Eat
You Alive!

Dear Diary:

Today in the school cafeteria I ate all my lunch . . as in everything on my tray. Why did I do that? I'm so stupid! Kevin called me a pig. Lisa brings her lunch, but she usually throws most of it away. I've also noticed that Shari doesn't eat much either.

How come I'm so hungry all the time?

Something must be wrong with me!

I'm gonna try reallyreallyreally hard to quit being such a pig!

Di:

    I did it again. I couldn't help it. I was so hungry, I ate the entire sandwich Mom packed in my sack lunch. All Lisa had was two baby carrots and a bunch of water.

    Cari said if I didn't watch it, I'd get fat.

    I'm really worried.

    And now that I'm home . . . and it's almost dinnertime . . . I'm hungry again.

    I've gotta figure out a way not to be hungry at breakfast, lunch, and dinner!

Okay, Di!

I finally figured it out. I saw Lisa taking pills this morning before first period. She says they're diet pills, and they'll keep you from getting hungry.

I asked her if I could have one, but she only has two left and didn't wanna give 'em up. Next time Mom takes me to the store, I'm gonna grab a pack. This is great. Now I'll stop being hungry and start to eat less, like Lisa and Shari.

How Much Do You Know?

Mom, are you as tuned in to nutrition as you need to be to help a growing, developing daughter? Let's test your knowledge before we jump into this all-important chapter on eating disorders, okay?

Weight a Minute

BY JENNIFER ELLIS

Find out if you really know the facts about gaining and losing pounds.

Glamour magazines, movies, and books often tell us that being attractive means being thin.

Guess what? That's a lie—don't let your daughter fall for it! Unfortunately, lots of people *believe* this lie, and sometimes they let it take over their lives.

In fact, most teen girls are on constant diets. Girls as young as 7 and 8 years old say that they're trying to lose weight. Sure, it's important to be healthy, but sometimes people go to an extreme and put themselves in danger.

So, come on, moms! Take this quiz and find out how much you know or *don't* know about food, exercise, and eating disorders.

t / f 1. Many healthy people think they need to lose weight.

t / f 2. A healthy diet means avoiding fat completely.

t / f 3. Fasting is a quick, easy way to lose weight.

t / f 4. It's possible to exercise too hard.

t / f 5. More than 90 percent of dieters gain back the weight they lose.

t / f 6. The thinner you are, the healthier you are.

t / f 7. People with eating disorders are always very thin.

t / f 8. If a food is fat-free, it won't cause you to gain weight.

t / f 9. Drinking water raises your metabolism.

t / f 10. People with eating disorders are always female.

t / f 11. Eating disorders are no big deal.

ANSWERS:

1. True. We get so many messages about being as thin as possible that sometimes it's hard to tell a *healthy* weight from an *unhealthy* one. Before you or your daughter try to lose weight, talk to your doctor.

2. False. We need to eat *some* fat so our bodies can work properly. Fat is a problem only if you're eating too much of it, or if you're eating the wrong kind. Look for foods with a low amount of saturated fat. Ask your doctor how much fat you need.

3. False. Fasting is probably the *worst* way to lose weight! When you deny yourself food, your body thinks you're starving, and it begins to store fat. This makes your metabolism—or the speed at which your body uses calories—go down. You'll actually lose weight more slowly and will gain it back quickly when you stop fasting.

4. True. If you exercise at a level that's too high, you may be doing yourself more harm than good. When you exercise, your body should feel like it's working hard, but you should be able to breathe easily and talk out loud. If you're gasping for air, you need to slow down.

5. True. Most people who diet gain back the weight when they quit. That starts a yo-yo cycle: They go on a diet, gain the weight back, and then diet again. The best way to lose weight and keep it off is to eat healthy foods and to exercise regularly.

6. False. Healthy people come in all shapes and sizes. You can't tell how healthy people are by how much they weigh.

7. False. Some people with eating disorders have anorexia, which means they are literally starving themselves. But other kinds of eating disorders affect people of all sizes. Some examples of this are overeating and bulimia. People with bulimia force themselves to vomit after eating. This can cause serious damage to their stomach, throat, and teeth.

8. False. You've probably seen food everywhere with the label "Fat-Free" in big letters across the front. This can be deceptive. It might say that the product doesn't contain *fat*, but it could still contain *sugar*, which turns itself into

fat if your body doesn't use it all.

9. True. Water is great for your body, and it *does* speed up your metabolism. You should drink about eight glasses of water every day. Also, remember to drink plenty of water while you exercise.

10. False. Teen girls are most associated with eating disorders, but the number of boys developing the same kinds of problems is growing. All sorts of people feel pressured to live up to an impossible ideal.

11. False. Eating disorders can be deadly. People who suffer from these problems are slowly killing themselves. If you become obsessed with your weight, talk to someone about it before it gets out of control.

The best way to maintain a good weight for your body type is to have a healthy lifestyle. Learn about nutrition and experiment with different kinds of exercise. Help your daughter take the focus off of how much she weighs, and teach her how to feel good about herself. Remind your daughter that she'll have her body for the rest of her life, so she'll want to take good care of it in a sensible manner. She's totally worth it![1]

Everyone's Thinking about Weight!

No doubt about it, eating disorders (anorexia and bulimia) affect thousands of teenage girls (and the number of affected boys is rapidly climbing) throughout the nation.

Moms, please be extrasensitive to your daughter's weight and eating habits. No, you don't want her filling up on junk food . . . but please know that any negative remarks you make about her weight during these teen years has the potential to scar her for life.

The goal? Teach her healthy eating habits so she'll learn how to make wise food choices. I can't tell you how many teen girls I'm around who think a good diet is: (1) simply not eating, (2) only eating a candy bar or a small bag of chips, or (3) filling up on microwave light popcorn and a diet soda.

If your daughter wants to lose weight, and you don't think she needs to, ask her about it. Why does she want to lose weight? Is she being pressured because she eats healthy? Is she simply eating all her food (school cafeterias are required to have certified professionals who make sure each lunch is filled with normal and nutritional portions) during lunch and being made fun of because of it?

MOMS, DON'T JUMP!

My fear is that some of you will read this and think, *Oh, no! My daughter has an eating disorder!* Please don't jump to conclusions, moms.

Your daughter may have eaten half a bag of cookies while she was cleaning her room or a bag of chips while studying for her science quiz. She may have even gained eight pounds this year. None of that means she has an eating disorder.

During her teen years, her body needs more food because it's changing and growing. She *needs* additional nourishment. If she's hungry, don't say anything damaging to her like, "Are you sure you want to eat that?" or, "How can you still be hungry?"

If she's involved in athletics or dance, she's burning extra calories during the day anyway, and she needs to replace them with extra food.

What you *don't* want is to call attention to your daughter's weight. Don't allow her to become obsessive about it. If you're concerned about what she *is* or *isn't* eating, consult a nutritionist before you say *anything* to your daughter.

It could be that she's *saying* she wants to lose weight, but what she really *means* is that she wants to get in shape. Those are two different things. Consider joining the Y.M.C.A. or a local fitness club with her. This would be a fantastic thing for the two of you to do together.

Janet knows her daughter struggles with her weight. To make sure Tami doesn't become obsessed with working out or excessive exercise, Janet goes to the fitness center *with* her daughter. Tami doesn't know this, but Janet is actually helping her daughter maintain a healthy balance.

What Kind of Mirror Are You?

Mom, your daughter is watching you. Are you setting a healthy example for her? Does she see you munching on chips, cupcakes, and candy bars? Do you strive to cook nutritional meals for your family, or do you find yourself casually calling for a pizza delivery a couple of times each week?

> *"Mom, don't try to help me with my homework unless you really know what you're doing."*
>
> Victoria, fifteen

On the other hand, if you're only eating an apple for dinner, she's receiving a nonverbal message that it's okay not to have vegetables and a complete meal.

Your daughter needs a healthy diet, and she also needs to see you as her role model. Strive to set a positive example *not only* by what you say to her (and again, be extremely selective in what you verbalize regarding her weight) but also by your lifestyle and what you serve your family for breakfast, lunch, and dinner.

How Do I Know?

If you suspect your daughter has an eating disorder, watch closely for the following warning signs:

Anorexia Nervosa
- Loss of menstrual period
- Dieting with enthusiasm when not overweight
- Claiming to feel "fat" when overweight is not a reality
- Preoccupation with food, calories, nutrition, and/or cooking
- Denial of hunger
- Excessive exercising, being overly active
- Frequent weighing
- Strange food-related behaviors
- Complaints of feeling bloated or nauseated when eating normal amounts of food
- Intermittent episodes of "binge eating"

Bulimia Nervosa
- Excessive concern about weight
- Strict dieting followed by eating binges
- Frequent overeating, especially when distressed
- Binge eating on high-calorie, sweet food
- Expressing guilt or shame about eating
- Use of laxatives and/or vomiting to control weight
- Leaving for the bathroom or disappearing after meals (secretive vomiting)

- Being secretive about binges and vomiting
- Planning binges or opportunities to binge
- Feeling out of control
- Depressive moods

Overcoming Eating Disorders

I want to introduce you to some special friends of mine. You'll be amazed at their openness and vulnerability. They are committed to being honest with me—and with you—about a battle they're fighting. Unfortunately, this battle is all too common among teen girls. It's the war of eating disorders. It can kill our daughters!

Remuda Ranch in Wickenburg, Arizona, is one of the top treatment centers in America for eating disorders. Mr. and Mrs. Ward Keller founded this Christian organization when they discovered their own teen daughter was struggling with an eating disorder.

Because I receive numerous letters from girls caught in this particular struggle, I decided to visit Remuda Ranch. I spoke in their morning chapel, and some of the girls agreed to talk very openly with me about their eating disorders.

Remuda Ranch wants to protect the girls' privacy, so I can't use the girls' last names. But to give you an insider's view of what the good battle is all about, the girls said you could eavesdrop on our conversation.

Why would they do this? Because they really want moms to understand this devastating battle. Please, moms, listen carefully.

How do your friends and family react to your eating disorder?
Olivia: We receive so many "get well" cards in the mail. You know, stuff that says, "Get better soon." It's not like we're *ill*.

Sometimes they'll say, "It's so sad when people come down with illnesses. It's a good thing yours is curable." But it's much deeper than that.

Mindy: And it makes you feel a lot of guilt. It's like there are so many people with horrible, untreatable diseases. Then here we are with eating disorders—and it *is* curable—but it's not that easy. It really *is* deeper than that.

Caroline: Yeah. I get letters from friends who say, "I can't wait till you get back and we can go out and eat all three meals."

Mindy: This is my second term at Remuda. When I went home last time, everyone expected me to be all healed and

> "Sometimes, Mom, when I'm in a bad mood and you're trying to find out what's wrong, it just makes it worse. Give me some space and time."
>
> Jacki, seventeen

just be the old Mindy. You know what the first thing we did was? Right when I got home, my whole family went out to eat. It was so scary! They expect it to be all gone, and it's not. I'll be fighting this the rest of my life. It's something I have to learn to deal with—but I can definitely fight it.

Why do teen girls develop eating disorders?

Mindy: My eating disorder started because I'd always been known as the perfect little girl who'd never do anything wrong—someone who had no problems. My family was the "perfect family." So this was kind of my way of going, "Ha, Ha! I'm *not* perfect. Look at me! If you think I'm perfect, just look—I'm not!" It was major rebellion on my part.

Caroline: For me, it's something I can control. I'm sixteen years old, and I feel like everything else in my life is being controlled by others. I have a twin sister, and she had an eating disorder when we were in fifth grade. I felt like second best. So, I also have to admit that this has been something to get attention as well as control.

Megan: For me, it was perfectionism—trying to be the perfect little girl. I've always been known as the bouncy, friendly girl of the high school, and I not only felt like I had to live up to my expectations and my high standards, but I'm such a people pleaser that I'd do anything to make people happy.

> *"Hey, Mom! Please understand that I like to be with my friends during hard times. Sometimes it's just easier to talk to them. Please don't misinterpret this as I love you less or don't need you."*
>
> *Brianna, eighteen*

I felt like I had to have the perfect body to go along with the perfect personality. I'd never show people how I really felt. Even if I was having the worst day, I'd put on that friendly "I'm-okay" mask.

You kind of lose your identity when you have an eating disorder, because when you start getting into recovery, you start seeing how you really are. You become yourself again. When you're in the eating disorder, it becomes your identity. It becomes who you are. That's why it's hard to give it up when you've had it for so long.

Mindy: Yeah. When I'm back at home, I'm known as "Mindy, the anorexic." That's my identity.

Megan: Whenever I get home, I'm afraid that I'll be seen as "the anorexic coming home," and I don't want to be treated like that, because things are better now. *Life* is better now.

Shayla: When I was in the third grade, kids called me "fat girl" and teased me relentlessly. So I started feeling ashamed of my body. I'd go home and stand in front of my mirror, telling myself that I wasn't good enough.

My brother and I went through a chunky stage at the same time. But when he entered high school and got involved in sports, he lost weight and got a lot of recognition for it. Since no one was complimenting me on anything, the feeling that I wasn't good enough was multiplied.

I started dieting, lost the weight, and finally got the recognition I wanted. I was about thirteen years old then, and that's when I slipped into the anorexia part. At this point the doctors were telling me I had to do this and that to gain weight, so I still felt as though I wasn't good enough. So then I slipped into compulsive eating, started getting teased again, and became bulimic. I'm sixteen now and just want to be well.

Anything specific your friends can do to help?

Caroline: Friends need to realize that it's not, "Let's go get something to eat, and that'll make it all better." Even if we *do* start eating, we still have the whole emotional thing to deal with.

Instead of a friend approaching me with, "Hey, let's go get a chocolate shake!" it would help so much more for that friend to simply come up and hug me.

Shayla: I think the most important thing friends need to realize is that an eating disorder is generally not all about food. It's usually an emotional problem. Somewhere along the line we've thought we've been rejected or hurt, and we think it was our fault. So we want to make ourselves better and perfect.

With society the way it is—and even with our peers at school—we tend to think that the perfect body will make us accepted, which means we won't have to feel the hurt. So we fight the food. It may *look* physical, but it's actually an emotional problem.

Mindy: Last time when I got home, people were assuming I was all better, and they'd say, "Okay, Mindy! Let's go out and eat!" Sure. I'd go eat with them, but as soon as we ate, I'd just go to the bathroom and throw up.

They thought since I was eating, everything was okay. But I was still hurting so bad inside, and nobody was asking about the hurt. No one really cared about my emotional side, because my physical side appeared to be okay.

Friends who truly listen, and friends who are just there, are really helpful. But I'd want to smack the people who'd come up to me saying, "You've got to get some meat on your bones now!"

Olivia: I think the most important thing friends can do to help is simply spend time with us—letting us know they care. We need to know that we don't have to live up to certain expectations. Comments like, "Your hair looks nice" are encouraging and helpful. Not, "Your hair looks nice *today*." That makes me wonder what it looked like yesterday!

Megan: A lot of us tend to judge ourselves on our looks and our body, and you know what? We're really cheating ourselves. I'm learning that what's on my inside is so much more important than what my outside looks like.

But society focuses so much on looks. It's everywhere. Instead of being complimented on what we're wearing or what we look like, it would be so much easier if friends would compliment us on a characteristic. For instance, instead of commenting on our jeans, hair, or shoes, why not mention friendly, caring, or sensitive? That's what's really important.

Mindy: Another thing that helps is just having friends who stick with you. I've had an eating disorder for three years, and I've lost so many friends. I barely have any friends at home anymore.

Caroline: Yeah. It's easy to become isolated. When you lose your friends because you're not doing anything fun with them anymore, you kind of just want to sit at home.

Mindy: All you do is lie around the house thinking about what you're going to eat next or what you're not going to eat and how you're going to burn the calories.

Megan: Even when I was with my friends, mentally I wasn't there. I wouldn't really be interacting with the group. I'd be thinking, *What am I going to order for dinner now that I'm here with ten girls?*

Or if we were all at a slumber party and they were eating pizza, I'd just be sitting there worrying over what I could eat and not be noticeable.

Mindy: It's like you're sitting in a room and there's a window that's separating you from everybody else. You can see them and touch them, but there's this imaginary wall. You can't level with

ISSUES THAT MAY CAUSE AN EATING DISORDER

—Low self-esteem, inadequacy, anxiety

—Definition of *self* in terms of appearance

—Actually being overweight

—Helplessness and need for control

—Difficulty in managing emotions

—Social anxiety and lack of social skills

—Fear of growing up

—Dysfunctional home life

—Lack of love or acceptance

them, because you're not there. It's like you're just watching everybody else.

For so long I felt like I was invisible. You're there watching everyone else, and you can't live.

What are some noticeable signs that someone is battling an eating disorder?

Megan: Withdrawal. Even all my friends would say, "Megan, you're just not Megan any more."

Caroline: Even my sister started telling me I wasn't the same. You act different. Your whole personality changes. You're not as fun as you used to be. You're also not as talkative or interactive with others.

Mindy: Another warning sign is going to the bathroom right after eating. Chances are, we're throwing up what we just ate. Denial is also a sign. Saying, "I've already eaten" is a huge cop-out.

> "Just because I talk to a guy on the phone and hang out with him and think about him a lot doesn't mean I love him!"
>
> Christine, fourteen

We're also very manipulative. Don't assume simply because we're eating and *not* going to the bathroom immediately afterward that everything's okay. I'd be eating with my parents and stuff the food under the table at a restaurant or drop it on the floor.

Shayla: And watch for mood swings.

Olivia: Another sign that someone may have an eating disorder is her bra size will drop.

Mindy: Malnutrition really affects your brain. You become very tired and irritable. It's hard even to concentrate. At school, I'd just sit at my desk and stare at the teacher, trying so hard to understand, but I just couldn't do it. I finally had to quit going to school because it was pointless. I couldn't sit still for an hour and a half. I couldn't do my work. I couldn't even *think*. It was horrible!

What are some of the dangers of eating disorders?

Mindy: It's not only dangerous, it's really selfish. I have a lot of guilt, because for the past three years my brother's been denied so many things he's wanted because half of our money has been devoted to "Mindy in treatment," "Mindy in counseling," and "Mindy's hospital bills."

Right before I went to my first treatment center, he yelled, "Why do you have to be so selfish? Mindy, you're taking all these things that we need just because you're stubborn!"

It really hurt. I'm not a selfish person, but what he said made sense.

I was hospitalized for calcium deficiency, because I had almost hit rock bottom from purging. I was hooked up to IVs, and the doctors told my parents that I could die. My brother called and said he had gone to the bookstore and picked out a poem to read at my eulogy.

That scared me—but the funny thing is, when you're in an eating disorder so thick, you don't realize how serious or dangerous or selfish it is. It's easy to rationalize and convince yourself that it's no big deal.

Shayla: Eating disorders can be slow suicide or instant death. With anorexics, they can have heart failure when they get to a low enough weight. With bulimics, they can rupture their esophagus when they're purging. That can be instant death.

How important is counseling to survive an eating disorder?

Olivia, Megan, Caroline, Shayla, Mindy: It's a must!

Olivia: But you have to be at the point where you *want* to get well.

What are some of the most frustrating things you struggle with in dealing with an eating disorder?

Olivia: It's tough when people tell you just to pray harder. I hear, "God is always with you." Yeah, I know He is. I *know* that. But simply knowing that doesn't help.

Mindy: I was at the point where I couldn't even pray. I couldn't open my Bible, couldn't go to church. I just felt so distant from God. Part of me wanted to be with God so badly, because I knew He could heal me. But the other part was like, "Stay away from God, because He will heal you." Yeah, I know. It's a huge contradiction, isn't it?

Hey, you *can* get help. There *is* hope! I'm getting so close to God now, and I'm finally getting back to the "old Mindy."

Shayla: How your friends react can also be tough. Everybody at school knows about my eating disorder, because I've had it for a few years. I'll be talking with a few of my friends about the struggles I'm having, and it seems like they're trying to one-up me on it. It's like, "I've done that before," and I'm thinking, *Guys, this isn't a popularity contest or ANY contest! It's a real, serious, life-or-death emotional problem.* It's so frustrating because they don't realize how dangerous it is. None of them has ever been to a treatment center.

You all agree that counseling is necessary to win this battle.

Olivia: Right. But again, you have to be at the point where you *want* to get well.

Mindy: I was so stubborn and so set on not getting better that I'd sit for an hour and a half with my therapist and all I'd talk about was, like, how bad I hated school. I'd sit there playing with a glitter stick while she was talking, and she began to tell me how I was a medical risk and needed to go somewhere. I can still see it now: It was morning, I had my bib overalls and a hat on. And I just sat there—pulled the hat over my head and played with the glitter stick—just wasting all that time.

Shayla: Outpatient help works for some people, but a lot of parents and friends think, *Just take her to a nutritionist, teach her how to eat, and she'll be okay.*

But it takes so much more than that. Think about it: If you're just going to a therapist once a week for an hour, you're not going to be able to get to the root of the problem, and the root is usually emotional.

Caroline: I couldn't help but notice all the fun my sister was having going out with her friends and being normal. I felt like life was just passing me by because of this eating disorder, so I decided I no longer wanted to watch—I wanted to be a part of life. And that means wanting to get well.

Mindy: I got to the point where my therapist finally told my parents that I had to go somewhere or she wasn't going to see me anymore. I was like, *Well, yeah, part of me wants to get better, but there's still that side of me that's like* huh-uh.

But once you decide you really want help, you begin to notice people who are living again, and you start to believe that you *can* get through this. Right now I'm, "Bring me the world! I want it!"

Have you experienced any physical dangers due to your eating disorder?

Megan: Yes. When a person makes herself throw up, she's really harming her body. I'd throw up as little as three pretzels.

Shayla: I took laxatives and diet pills. The laxatives caused a lot of cramping. I'd pass out from so much pain. And you know what? It doesn't really work. I mean, the laxatives pass food through you, but the weight you lose is water. So by the time you drink a glass of water, it's all coming back.

Mindy: I was so scared of the five calories in gum that I'd start spitting out the gum as soon as I had it in my mouth.

I was in school when my esophagus went into spasms. The tube that connected my esophagus to my stomach was really rough, and all the tissue in it was all messed up. The acid kept coming up and stayed in my chest. I felt like I was having a heart attack. When I went into shock, my vice principal carried me to my dad's car, and they rushed me to the emergency room. That was a major smack in the face that made me want to get better.

Because of the lack of potassium in my body, my toes and hands would curl up. It's really frightening to be sitting in school and not be able to straighten them out! My leg muscles would get really tight and throbby, and my joints ached a lot. That was due to low calcium.

See, there's so much that happens to the body when we start to mistreat it and deprive it of the nutrients it needs. Your bones get osteoporosis if you don't have enough calcium. When you take laxatives, you mess up the electrolytes in your body. And when you throw up, you're messing up your esophagus. It's not worth it!

Shayla: You can also harm your body from too much exercise. I was exercising three hours a day.

Mindy: When I arrived here at Remuda, I was throwing up everything. If I even put on lipstick, I'd run to the bathroom; I'd make sure that nothing had any calories in it. It was horrible. I wouldn't even brush my teeth because I was afraid the toothpaste might have a few calories in it!

At this point, another teen girl joins our conversation. Meet Alicia.

Alicia: I'm seventeen, and like a lot of others, for me it's a control thing. Food is a thing I can control when I'm upset or lonely or feeling rejected. I was a big binger.

I'd go to five fast-food restaurants in a row. Here's how it worked: I'd never go through the entrance. I'd use the drive-through because it's less embarrassing. I'd pull up at Burger King and order two veggie Whoppers, two large fries, and a milkshake. I'd eat all that then throw it up and go to Taco Bell and start over. I spent around fifty dollars a day binging on food.

I'd weigh myself fifteen times a day. Because I didn't want any added weight from even my shoelaces, I'd take everything off before stepping on the scales. And if I

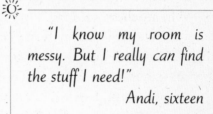

"I know my room is messy. But I really can find the stuff I need!"

Andi, sixteen

thought I weighed too much, I'd take sixty laxatives. When I started taking laxatives, four or five would be enough, but that didn't last long. My body soon got used to that, and I had to increase the amount to twenty. Then when that amount no longer worked, I went to sixty.

I'd literally be going to the bathroom all night long. Mom would find me passed out on the floor in the hall because I was so dehydrated, and I'd fall down while trying to walk back to my bedroom.

I eventually lost control of my bodily functions, because when you're dehydrated, it just comes out!

Many teen girls say, "I don't have an eating disorder; I just want to lose five pounds." Any advice for them?

Shayla: I'd encourage them to check it out with their doctor first. I'd tell them, Discuss your goal range—even consider talking with a nutritionist. Don't do it by yourself.

If your doctor says you don't need to lose five pounds, then don't do it, because if you're determined to go behind his back, chances are five pounds will never be enough for you. Your goal weight will change every day.

If you're feeling bad about how you look, and your doctor won't let you lose five pounds, you probably need to talk with a counselor and work on your self-esteem. I hope you can realize that it's the inside that counts. Five pounds isn't going to make your personality change for the better.

Alicia: And five pounds isn't going to change your body shape either. Your real friends will love you just as much with five more pounds. It doesn't matter.

What about the teen girl who's thinking, Hey, I'm not at a **treatment center! Those girls really have major problems. I'm not that bad.**

Mindy: I remember praying, "God, make me an anorexic," because I'd read magazine articles about eating disorders and I'd think, *Whatever. Imagine that! Somebody being* made *to gain weight!* And here I am, three years later, with an eating disorder. It's never enough—you never lose enough weight.

I was at my lowest weight, and it wasn't enough. You come here and see all these stick-skinny girls with tubes up their noses and they say, "I don't need a tube," and you can look at them and say, "Yes, you do!" Because it's never enough.

Olivia: If you can't eat normally, and if you can't go through your day without thinking about losing weight, then you should get help, because this is a serious thing! It ruins your life!

Losing pounds doesn't really do anything for you. When I was at my lowest weight, I didn't have any more friends than I do now. No one loved me any more. All they did was ask me what was wrong. I didn't feel any better about myself; I felt awful.

What is that tube you're wearing and that I see other girls here at Remuda wearing?

Mindy: It's a feeding tube. It's active at night.

Caroline: Girls who are really bad can't get enough calories at one time to gain weight—it would shock their system and could kill them. So they get them through a feeding tube that's turned on during their sleep. When they gain a certain amount of weight, then they start eating more real food. We call them "tubers."

What would you like to say to teen girls?

Shayla: If you have problems with food, go to a Christian therapist and take it straight to God. He made you the way you are for a reason. My saying around here is "You are one-hundred-percent perfect *you.*"

Megan: Don't judge yourself on what you look like. That's totally cheating yourself. There are so many more qualities that God gave you besides an outward appearance.

Alicia: An eating dis-order isn't just about the weight or the food. It goes a lot deeper. Oftentimes there's a lot of hurt some-one is trying to deal with—which proves that no matter how much weight you lose, it's not going to bring you happiness. Your true happiness will be found only in God.

> "If I want to talk about something, I will."
> Maya, seventeen

Meet some girls from another section of Remuda Ranch. These girls are still living at Remuda, but they're in an apartment, attending a local high school, and working to become strong enough to return to their homes and families.

Girls, you're kind of at a halfway point now. You're heading in the right direction, but you're still facing some battles. Please be honest about what you're experiencing and how you're getting your lives back together.

Heather: Okay. Well, this is my second time here, and the question is, "How can I assure everyone I'm not going to fall back again?" I can't say one hundred percent that I won't fall back, but right now I totally do *not* want to go back to the war of an eating disorder.

I think you truly have to hit rock bottom, where things have gotten so bad that you just have nothing else to live for. I hit that point my second time through. I'm so excited now to live life and to *have* a life besides an eating disorder.

> "Just because I don't want to talk doesn't mean I don't love you. I love you! Sometimes I just need to sort out all the stuff that's going on inside my head."
>
> Rashawna, eighteen

Paula: I went home last time and did well for about six months. I never had the intent of falling back. I never thought that would happen. But I was really young—I was only twelve, and it was really hard being away from home. I missed my family; my parents had a baby and I missed the birth—all kinds of stuff happened—and I just slipped back into it.

I have a strong support system this time. I still have the thoughts, but I don't have the actions that go along with the thoughts. I've realized that I worried about food so much! And I did it to get acceptance from others. But when I stop and think about it, *they* don't think about it twenty-four/seven, so why should I? I'm ready to go home and deal with life.

Heather: I think it's going to be a daily battle with the thoughts. I've gotten to the point where I'm living in what we call "partial" now. I'm not forced to eat meals, but since I've been in the apartment, my goal has been to eat regular meals consistently, because I've come to the point where I totally don't want this thing. Even though I might have a thought to restrict, or exercise, or whatever, I can remember how bad it was when I was into my eating disorder. I keep reminding myself that I don't want to go back to that.

I think once you're truly willing to give up your eating disorder, you can do it—but until you get to that point, it's going to be a really big struggle.

Jill: I don't know if I'm going to end up coming back here or not, but I don't think I've hit rock bottom with my eating disorder. I really don't want to come back. When I look at normal people, I think, *I wish I could be like them. I wish I could have a piece of cake without feeling yucky.*

The good thing is that I'm learning I can have a little bit of anything. The key is balance. And I also know I have God. I pray every time I struggle, and it really helps.

Heather: The way our society portrays bodies is sick. Everyone is just so skinny, so emaciated, and none of them looks happy anymore. When you see models in pictures, they never smile. Right now what society is telling us is normal really *isn't* normal!

Paula: And it's not just the secular side of society; oftentimes you'll find this in the Christian circles too. I was at a Christian club, and they had painted cool pictures on the wall with little bubble sayings. One of them was "Smile—you'll burn two calories." We need to know how to fend that off.

Heather: I just wish there were some magic thing we could say to encourage girls not even to start with an eating disorder. We're supposed to *live* life, not spend our days worrying about food and our bodies. If girls will simply eat a balanced diet and exercise a little bit, they'll be fine.

Jill: I've lost nearly three years out of my life. There's no way to go back and fix things again. I just have to pick myself up and go on. It's not worth it to be so distant from life for so long and then have to go to a treatment center.

Amanda: It's just not worth it! I lost six and a half months of my life when I could've been happy and having fun instead of being in a treatment center. I wish I could take those six and a half months back.

But it's exciting to see you allowing God to make good things happen out of this devastating disease!

Heather: Right. We need to focus on what we have to look forward to. There's so much more in life than body weight and who likes you and who doesn't!

You're on the upper side of recovery and planning to return to your families soon. Any final thoughts for other teen girls battling eating disorders?

Heather: It's so much easier just to eat three meals a day than go through what we've battled. Please don't start skipping that first meal. It can easily turn into a downward spiral. Eat balanced meals, and live your life to the fullest!

More Information on Eating Disorders

Remuda Ranch offers the following questions for your daughter as a guide to discern whether she has an eating disorder.

Eating Disorder Symptoms
❏ Do you have eating habits that are different from those of your family or friends?

❏ Do you prefer to eat alone?

❏ Do you avoid social occasions that involve eating?

❑ Do your friends or family tell you that you are too thin or underweight?

❑ Do you see yourself as "fatter" or bigger than your friends?

❑ Is it important for you to be thinner than all your friends?

❑ Has your menstrual period ceased or become irregular?

❑ Do you spend a lot of time thinking or worrying about what you're going to eat or what you cannot eat?

❑ Do you spend a lot of time thinking about your weight or body shape?

❑ Would you panic if you found you had gained two pounds?

❑ Do you weigh yourself more than twice a week?

❑ Do you avoid weighing yourself?

❑ Do you get angry when people tell you what to eat?

❑ Do you get angry when people ask you what you have eaten?

❑ Do you keep your fears about food and eating to yourself because you are afraid no one will understand?

❑ Do you enjoy cooking for others but don't allow yourself to eat what you fix?

❑ Is the most powerful fear in your life the fear of gaining weight or becoming fat?

❑ Does losing weight cause you to feel better about yourself and everything in your life?

❑ Does weight gain cause you to feel like a failure or hopeless about your life?

❑ Do you go a day or longer without eating as a means of weight control?

❑ Do you vomit as a means of weight control?

❏ Do you use laxatives or diuretics as a means of weight control?

❏ Do you exercise as a means of weight control?

❏ Do you exercise more than five times a week or more than one hour a day?

❏ Do you find yourself panicking about gaining weight if you cannot exercise?

❏ Do you spend time reading books and articles about nutrition, dieting, or exercise?

❏ Are you a perfectionist?

❏ Are you ever satisfied with yourself or your performance?

❏ Do you find yourself binging uncontrollably on large amounts of food to the point where you feel sick?

❏ Do you eat all day long regardless of whether you are hungry?

❏ Do you find yourself eating when going through stressful periods of time?

❏ Do you start new diets constantly?

Remuda Ranch uses the following eating disorder screen before admitting a patient to its facility.

Remuda's Adolescent Eating Disorder Screen

❏ Do you feel sick when you sit down at the table?

❏ Are you afraid to touch any foods?

❏ Do you eat your foods in a certain order?

❏ Do you have a different view of your body than other people do?

❏ Do you prefer to eat by yourself?

❏ Do your family and friends "bug" you about what you eat?

❏ Does anyone tell you that you spend too much time in physical activity?

❏ Do you get upset if something isn't perfect?

❏ Do you tear your food into tiny pieces before eating it?

❏ Are you afraid to be seen in public in a swimsuit?

❏ Do you avoid certain foods because you think they are going to change the way you look?[2]

If you answered yes to several of the above, you may have or may be developing an eating disorder. Please let someone know.

For more information on eating disorders, please contact:

Remuda Ranch
Programs for Anorexia and Bulimia
One East Apache
Wickenburg, AZ 85390
1-800-445-1900
remuda@goodnet.com
http://www.remuda-ranch.com

☼ *Wrapping It Up* ☼

Mom, do you realize that at this particular time in your daughter's life, you have the power to make or break how she sees herself? It's true! Every girl in the world yearns for her mother's unconditional acceptance. When she receives *unconditional* acceptance—regardless of grades, weight, looks, or personality—she begins the process of accepting herself.

Please don't take for granted the tremendous amount of molding and shaping power you have right now. There *will* come a time when you won't have it. So use what you have got in a positive way to build your daughter up, encourage her, and be positive toward her!

Father, I don't want to say or do the wrong thing with my daughter. Please help me realize how powerful my words are. Father, I speak so often without stopping first to consider how my words will affect her. Please break me of that habit.

Teach me to think first and speak last. Years from now, I want her to look back on her life in my home and remember my words and actions as positive, healthy, and encouraging. Help me to help her establish a good image of herself.

Amen.

☼ *Memorize It . . . with Your Daughter* ☼

Woe to him who quarrels with his Maker. . . . Does the clay say to the potter, "What are you making?"

Does your work say, "He has no hands?"

Woe to him who says to his father, "What have you begotten?" or to his mother, "What have you brought to birth?" (Isaiah 45:9–10)

What's the Problem? Take It to Christ!
Helping Your Teen Daughter Take Her Problems to Christ
Can Set a Positive Course for Years to Come

It's Monday, and your fourteen-year-old daughter, Tawni, doesn't want to go to school. She's facing a crisis. Her fourth-period history teacher intimidates her. Tawni interprets this as hostility.

Monday evening she refuses supper. "Jenna ignored me all day at school," she says. Crisis.

Tuesday afternoon you find out she's feeling guilty because Emily talked her into helping her cheat on the English pop quiz. Crisis.

Wednesday morning, Tawni announces she has a zit the size of a volcano on her forehead. Her bangs cover her forehead, but even when she pulls them up to prove the disaster, you have trouble locating the blemish. She begs to be excused from school. Crisis.

Wednesday evening, she says Jason is saying ugly things about her, and Ryan spread the rumors to Julie and Sarah. Crisis.

When you're a teen girl, every day can be a crisis. No—make that every *hour*. Because of fluctuating hormones and other physiological changes, her world can explode with anything as diverse as not being able to find her favorite pair of jeans to forgetting a homework assignment to not being invited to Amy's party to losing her notebook to Eric not saying hi to her between classes.

Congratulations!

Wow! What an incredible opportunity.

What?

Imagine, if you can teach your daughter to take her daily crises to God *now*—during her teen years—chances are she'll be seeking answers from her heavenly Father a few years from now when her fiancé walks out on her, she doesn't get into law school, or she begins to question truth.

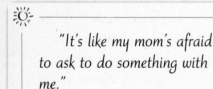

"It's like my mom's afraid to ask to do something with me."

Taryn, fourteen

As adults, we know the ultimate answer— that God can use our problems to strengthen us and to draw us closer to Him. But when you're fourteen and you've tried for three weeks to get Brett's attention and he *still* doesn't know you exist, being "strengthened" doesn't sound too attractive.

Game Plan

But God cares about Tawni's feelings. He understands exactly how she feels when Brett doesn't return her smile. *You* know that. And your teen probably knows that too—somewhere deep inside. But rather than simply providing a good answer she can offer in Sunday school, our goal is to help her take that truth and attach it to her lifestyle.

Think of it this way: When your daughter cuts herself, she automatically reaches for a Band-Aid. Because she's done this for years, it has almost become a natural reflex. She doesn't need to stop and *think* about the bandage; she just opens the medicine cabinet and grabs one.

Though right now your daughter won't naturally look for an opportunity to deepen her spiritual roots when she's in the midst of a crisis, with the right game plan, you *can* steer her toward making that a reality.

How? Glad you asked. Let's talk strategy.

Be a model. The best way to teach your daughter that God can handle every problem she faces is to live that truth yourself. When *you* face a crisis, how do *you* respond? Does she see you turn to the Word? Does she catch you on your knees? Do you continue to exhibit a positive attitude in the midst of pain? Do you model the possibility that your problem may actually be a blessing in disguise?

Be willing to teach your daughter how to turn to God in a crisis. And be willing to teach through example—your own life.

Be a prayer warrior. When your daughter is facing a crisis, she needs your ears. The Holy Spirit will help you discern when to offer advice and when simply to listen. But she also needs the ears of her heavenly Father. So take her to the throne.

Meet her in her own turf—on the edge of her bed, on the floor in front of the TV, at the kitchen table—wherever she's comfortable. Kneel with her. *What's the magic in kneeling?* No magic—but it sure helps us quickly grab the proper perspective. It's as if you're saying to your daughter, "We're kneeling in humility with this problem. We feel overwhelmed. But we serve a giant God, and we're taking it straight to Him. Prayer is serious business. God really cares!"

And after you've prayed *together,* continue to pray about her problem on your own—or with your spouse. Drop a note in her lunch sack the next morning: "Dad and I are praying about [name specific problem] today."

Steer her to Scripture. Show her how to use a concordance, and read specific verses with her that tell us how to handle problems. You might want to jot a few of her favorites on some three-by-five cards and put them inside her notebook.

Some suggested scriptures to get you started: James 1:1–4; 1 Peter 1:7; 1 Peter 4:1–2; 1 Peter 5:7–10; and 2 Corinthians 4:7–9.

Bring the big picture into focus. As adults, we know that zit on Tawni's forehead really *isn't* a crisis. And the hostile teacher from another planet may simply be hard because he cares about challenging his students. And though Brett doesn't know who she is, Doug *did* call twice this week.

We have the ability to see the big picture, but teens have to be *taught* to see it. Without belittling her crisis, dissect the problem with her. Help her bring it into perspective. Guide your daughter to a realistic view of life's disappointments.

Her Adult Life

And the big picture right now? If you can teach your teen girl to turn to God—almost as a natural reflex—the habit will stay with her the rest of her life. Anyone can turn to Christ when her back is against the wall. Our daughters have a much higher calling. God wants their dependence *before* their world explodes.

Classroom
Challenges

Hey, Di!

I don't get Mr. Hildebrand. I actually entered biology class this year enjoying it. But lately he's totally been on my case. And you know . . . as I think back on it . . . I'm pretty sure it all started a couple of days after I stood at the flagpole with some of my other Christian friends early one morning to pray for our school.

Anytime I raise my hand to get into the class discussion, he interrupts me, or laughs at me, or tears my theories apart. Yesterday I got back a test with a question marked wrong that was really correct. When I asked him about it later, he said, "Your handwriting was too hard to read. If I can't read it, you don't get credit for the answer."

GIMME A BREAK!

What gives?

Di:

Today I got back my paper on abortion. I worked for two weeks on that and was really proud of it. I got a C-minus. A C-minus! I really think Hildebrand's out to get me.

I know we have opposing views on the subject . . . but this is ridiculous. I gave fact after fact about how the unborn fetus really is a human life and how no one has the right to end that life except God.

And with that red pen of his, he marked all through my paper, saying stuff like, "Every woman should have a choice" and, "You're being too close-minded" and on and on.

I tried to talk with him after class, but he said he didn't appreciate my narrow-mindedness and I'd better get to my next class.

What is this?

I feel like I'm being persecuted for my beliefs!

Believe It — It's Happening

Persecution against Christians in public schools, colleges, and universities *does* exist. Your daughter could very easily become a victim of classroom persecution during the next few years. How will you help her deal with it? Should she argue, simply take it, or complain to a higher authority?

First, you need a strategy. Don't go into the battle blinded and unprepared. Do your homework.

Know the facts. Make sure your statistics are correct. Be willing to spend the amount of time necessary to do the research you need.

State the facts. After you *have* the necessary information, don't be afraid to stand up and share the truth. After all, if you have documentation, there's nothing to fear.

Maintain a positive attitude. It's easy for a student to fall into the "fighting mode," especially if her teacher is already *in* that mode. Don't fall for it. Stay above an emotional level, and continue to present your facts on an intellectual platform.

Remain calm. Don't raise your voice or show anger. This could easily be used against you. Don't do anything that would give the persecutor more ammunition against you. Smile as you present your opposing view. Show a kind spirit through all you do.

It Happened to Me

I'll never forget the persecution I faced in graduate school. I attended the University of Central Oklahoma for a master's degree in creative writing. It was an excellent program, and I really enjoyed it. After a specific amount of classes, hours, and course-work, the completion of the degree was either a thesis, a book of poetry, a novel, or a script for a play. The professors brought in professional writers—artists-in-residence—to teach this final rotation of thesis options.

Since I was a high-school speech and drama teacher at the time, I decided to write a script. I thought I might be able to use it in my drama class someday. The scriptwriting class was a three-semester rotation taught by professional scriptwriters from New York who had written for television and/or live theater.

I was excited when I met the first artist-in-residence. *This guy really knows his stuff,* I thought. *By the time I have my master's degree, I'll also have a play that's good enough to be performed or published!*

There were about twenty-five adults in this night class that met weekly. Each week, we'd write a little more on our play, bring copies of it to class, and have it read aloud by classmates. My excitement quickly diminished as I listened to the first few pages of my peers' writing read aloud. Page after page was filled with dialogue laced with obscenities, God's name taken in vain, and sexual connotations. It was disgusting.

I was beginning to wonder how this class of adults would react to *my* writing. I was creating a play called *Starmaker,* which was a parable about Christ, the disciples, and the gospel. It was very unique. Very creative. Very original.

Now, keep in mind, I was writing it for possible production for my own drama students. It was filled with humor, creative dialogue, and lots of movement. I literally *saw* the entire production in my head as I wrote. I was having a blast!

Though my characters didn't use the name *God,* it was clear through obvious symbolism that Starmaker was God and the six main characters were the disciples. Throughout the production, they acted out my own twisted version of fairy tales, nursery rhymes, and stories found in Scripture to present God as being the One who died for our sins, rose again, and wanted to give us meaning and purpose through forgiveness of our sins.

It was cleverly done in such a way that it *could* be performed in a public-school setting. (It didn't even mention Jesus or as much Scripture as *Godspell*, which has been performed in thousands of high schools around the nation.)

But it also didn't contain any swearing or off-color language. I was thinking I'd probably be laughed out of the class against all the "real-life" language that filled everyone else's scripts.

A Turn of Events

To my surprise, the class *loved* it! They enjoyed reading it, laughed till their sides hurt, and couldn't wait for the next section the following week. The artist-in-residence who was teaching the class told me I had a real feel of the stage and a gift for dialogue. At the end of the semester, I received an A.

I excitedly signed up for the next semester and continued the script. Since many of the same students rolled over, as I did, to continue the class, they were already familiar with the script and were anticipating more. Our new artist-in-residence from New York didn't say much. He never encouraged me, but he did ask me a few questions. Each time, I answered with confidence. After all, I had prayed over the script and believed I was writing what Christ wanted me to write. I wanted to give a positive message through my work to the adults in the class, and to the students who would someday read my words. I received an A at the end of the semester.

"I wish my mom would order enough of my school pictures for my friends."

Sabrina, eleven

Only one more semester to go, and I'd have a completed two-and-a-half-hour production in my hand along with my master's degree. Again, I excitedly signed up for the third semester of script-writing class and noticed we had the same artist-in-residence from New York as we previously had for our second semester.

I continued to write, and the class continued to read. I finally finished the play and felt good about it. I had given it a year and a half of my life, and I knew it was good. It was funny, yet it had a message.

The artist-in-residence, knowing I would receive my master's degree at the completion of this course with his final approval of my script, called me into his office one evening. His words shocked me.

"Susie, I will not sign off on your script."

"Why?" I asked. "It's finished. I've completed everything I need for the course."

"Because I don't like it."

I was stunned. I didn't know he had to like it personally to give me the credit I deserved. "You . . . you don't like it?"

"No. I don't like it. I don't like religious stuff."

"But Jesus Christ is never even mentioned in the production."

"I don't care. It's obvious that's who it's about, and I don't like it."

"And I'm just now hearing about it?" I pressed.

"Look," he continued. "I gave you an A last semester, but I won't give you an A this time around."

"You *gave* me an A . . . or I *earned* an A?" I asked.

"Well, you got an A," he replied. "But you won't get one this time."

"But why?" I asked. "I don't understand."

"Look, Susie. The only kind of religious plays I like are the ones in which the Christians are killed in the end."

"I want my degree," I stated.

"Then you'll have to completely change the play."

I couldn't believe it!

I had done the work, and my work was good. But because he didn't like it, I wasn't going to get the grade I deserved, and I wasn't going to get his sign-off.

The graduate assistant for the class pulled me aside and told me I had created a masterpiece. "The dialogue is genius," she said. "And the way you've cleverly woven in so many different scenarios is incredible. I personally met with the artist-in-residence and told him he could *not* fail you when you had done such a good job with your script. He really wants to fail you, Susie.

"I point-blank asked him, 'Did she complete the assignment over the past three semesters?' He admitted you had. So I said, 'You can't do this! You can't fail her simply because you don't like what she wrote. If she's done the assignment correctly, you *have* to pass her.' "

I thanked the grad assistant but still didn't know what to do. After spending time in prayer, I decided not to compromise what I felt God had called me to write. I accepted the lower grade and didn't receive his sign-off.

Now I was at a standstill. I was frozen. All my coursework was completed. But I couldn't receive the degree until the visiting professor from my scriptwriting class would sign off on my play. All the time, money, and effort I had put into getting a master's degree was wasted.

God Always Has a Plan

I was pretty dejected. And hurt. I felt I had been beaten up. I was finally able to label it as persecution for my beliefs. And I simply gave it to God.

The following year, I received a call at home from the new artist-in-residence for a new rotation of scriptwriting classes. "Susie," he said, "I just arrived here a couple of weeks ago, and I'm going through some files in my office. I came across your script. It looks to me like you've completed everything you need to do. Let's schedule your oral examination and get you your master's degree. I've already signed off on your script."

Wow.

I was speechless.

God is faithful, isn't He? God is *faithful!*

In October of the following year, I resigned my teaching position to accept Focus on the Family's invitation to create a magazine for teen girls (now known as *Brio*). Before I left, though, the school brought in my replacement to work alongside me for my last two weeks.

As Mrs. Calhoun looked at the schedule, she noticed we'd be producing a play in the next few months. "Have you selected a play yet?" she asked.

I told her about the play I had written. "The students have read *Starmaker* and like it, and I was planning on producing it this semester. But here are several drama catalogs you can look through for other options. You have full authority to select any play you desire."

She took the script for *Starmaker* and the catalogs home with her and told

> "I wish my mom would get it that I don't like to talk about my period!"
> Shawnda, fourteen

me a few days later that she had chosen *Starmaker*.

"I love it," she said. "And since the students have already read through it, I want to produce it."

Yes, God is faithful.

I'm not the only person in America who has struggled with an unfair teacher or professor. Check out this true story that happened to a Christian teen girl during her high-school years.

PERSECUTION IN AMERICA?

BY ANGELA J. SMITH

What happens in some public schools is scary!
But you don't have to suffer alone!

Ms. Janet Rogers* stood 6 feet tall. Her 200-plus pounds accentuated her commanding voice. She made my high-school journalism class enjoyable—laughing with her students and allowing us to joke around.

She definitely had her favorites, and I was one of them. I could hold my own in our heated class discussions, and we enjoyed talking together. In November, she asked the class to write persuasive papers.

I chose the controversial topic of abortion. Knowing it was a well-written paper, I was surprised to see that my grade was a C when she handed it back.

Our next assignment was to write a paper on whether grade-school children should learn about gay and lesbian parents. Although not actively walking with the Lord at the time—as I am now—I wrote a very solid, Christian paper

that expressed my views based on the Bible.

My days of looking forward to class were over. I now dreaded what had become the longest 50 minutes of each day. Ms. Rogers made a malicious and cruel comment about me in front of the class every single day. Her put-downs ranged from, "I bet your parents wish they'd had an abortion when they saw you" to "Let's all get down and bow to such a good little Christian girl." The class always laughed.

More Surprises

In spite of the badgering, I worked hard all year, and to my surprise, I was chosen to be on the newspaper staff for the following school year.

It was all the hard work I expected, and I was determined to prove myself to Ms. Rogers. I

* *The name of the teacher at the school has been changed to protect the author and the teacher.*

worked twice as hard as everyone else to avoid any chance of being picked on. But she was relentless. I was a walking time bomb ready to explode.

Early that fall, my parents discovered I was bulimic. I was immediately put in counseling for my eating disorder. My parents' question to me was, "Why are you doing this?" In the first counseling session, I mentioned the stress I was facing at school, and the counselor encouraged me to tell my folks.

Dad immediately went to the school to confront Ms. Rogers. He threatened to go to the principal if she didn't apologize to me. She denied the accusations and began to treat me worse. Her comments were now spiced with swear words, punctuated with, "Did I say that *Christian* enough for you, Angela?"

The Battle Rages

Dad took my case to the school administration, and to my surprise our principal didn't believe a word I said. I was called in and asked to read the list of things she'd said. I could barely read through my tears as I struggled to complete the list. Each word brought more trauma as Ms. Rogers sat across the table staring coldly at me.

She denied everything, and I knew none of the students who had heard her comments—even my close friends—would support me and risk her wrath and retribution.

Does Time Really Heal?

January 18, 1993, was my last day at Riverview High School. It was where I lived and died, lost and won, fought and celebrated, and now would never return. Hours of counseling and rivers of tears have all passed.

It's hard for me even to drive by the school. The very thought of opening the large double doors and heading down the halls sends me into sheer panic. I haven't seen Janet Rogers since that day, although to my knowledge she's still employed at Riverview.

I know that many lawyers and school boards would love to hear my story, but my point is not to win money, fame, or even sympathy. My purpose is to educate others who may someday face a Janet Rogers.

While we have hundreds of excellent public school systems that would *not* allow this to happen to a student, the frightening reality is also that many middle-school and high-school students are being persecuted for their faith every day—not in Communist countries halfway across the world, but in the country that boasts of "freedom of religion," the United States of America. So what can you do if persecution happens to you?

Step 1: Tell your parents. Not even one or two negative comments about your faith or religion are allowed. For your own well-being, make sure your parents know the entire situation. I made the mistake of internalizing the problem, which led to an eating disorder, depression, and a bad relationship with my parents.

If I had been open with them from the very beginning about the struggle I faced at school, they could have helped me take action sooner. Telling *someone*— a youth pastor, counselor, close friend—is the first step to easing the problem.

Step 2: Talk it out. Whether your problem is with a teacher or another student, the best thing to do is tell the person directly that it bothers you, and that you want things to stop. Sometimes an inappropriate comment may simply be a case of having a big mouth or speaking too soon, so you may get an apology. Hopefully, the problem will end here.

Step 3: Write down what you've experienced. If the problem persists, start taking detailed notes of who said what, and when and where this took place. If you ever *do* decide to press charges, you'll need to have an exact account of what has taken place.

Step 4: Contemplate your options. If things continue or get worse, talk with your principal or school board. Make sure you bring a parent with you to help defend your integrity. The more support you have, the better.

Most of all, remember that in any situation the Lord is your constant advocate and ally. Ultimately, it's Jesus Christ they're persecuting.[1]

Your Daughter Does Have Rights

Mom, your daughter *does* have specific rights on her school campus. You may be familiar with the annual "See You at the Pole" event in which *millions* of students around the world stand together at their school flagpole one day in September before first period and pray for their schools and for each other.

I hear from students who tell me their principal came out and broke up the gathering or a teacher warned them not even to try it. Guess what? Your daughter has a constitutional *right* to stand at her school's flagpole and pray.

Please study the following rights and discuss them with your daughter. The more she understands what she *is* able to do on campus, the better equipped she'll be to take a stand.

Students' Bill of Rights
on a Public School Campus

1. **THE RIGHT to Meet with Other Religious Students.** The Equal Access Act allows students the freedom to meet on campus for the purpose of discussing religious issues.

2. **THE RIGHT to Identify Your Religious Beliefs through Signs and Symbols.** Students are free to express their religious beliefs through signs and symbols.

3. **THE RIGHT to Talk about Your Religious Beliefs on Campus.** Freedom of speech is a fundamental right mandated in the United States Constitution and does not exclude the schoolyard.

4. **THE RIGHT to Distribute Religious Literature on Campus.** Distributing literature on campus may not be restricted simply because the literature is religious.

5. **THE RIGHT to Pray on Campus.** Students may pray alone or with others so long as it does not disrupt school activities or is not forced on others.

6. **THE RIGHT to Carry or Study Your Bible on Campus.** The Supreme Court of the United States has said only that *state-directed* Bible reading is unconstitutional.

7. **THE RIGHT to Do Research Papers, Speeches, and Creative Projects with Religious Themes.** The First Amendment to the United States Constitution does not forbid all mention of religion in public schools.

8. **THE RIGHT to Be Exempt.** Students may be exempt from activities and class content that contradict their religious beliefs.

9. **THE RIGHT to Celebrate or Study Religious Holidays on Campus.** Music, art, literature, and drama that have religious themes are permitted as part of the curriculum for school activities if presented in an objective manner as a traditional part of the cultural and religious heritage of the particular holiday.

10. **THE RIGHT to Meet with School Officials.** The First Amendment forbids Congress to make any law that would restrict the right of the people to petition the government (school officials).[2]

☼ *Wrapping It Up* ☼

Whether your daughter attends a public or private school, or even if she's homeschooled, at some point in her life her faith will be challenged. I've heard that more Christians are facing persecution around the world right now than at any other time in history.

Let's equip our girls, first of all, with a strong, intimate relationship with Christ. And next, let's teach them how to articulate why they believe what they do.

Are you spending time in Bible reading and prayer with your daughter? If not, will you accept my challenge to do so? Your daughter needs your prayers and a godly relationship modeled in you more now than ever.

Father, things have changed so much since I walked through the hallways of school. I know my daughter is facing things I never had to encounter when I was her age; I'm just not always sure what those issues are.

Please show me how to develop an ongoing, close relationship with her, so she'll feel comfortable coming to me with the battles she encounters. Lord, help me to understand and be able to verbalize my faith more articulately. Show me how to take a strong stand for my beliefs, so my daughter will have the example she needs.

And above all, Father, help me to keep a positive and Christlike attitude even in the midst of my daughter's greatest battles. Use me to help her remember that You truly are our greatest advocate.

Amen.

☼ *Memorize It . . . with Your Daughter* ☼

Remember the words I spoke to you: "No servant is greater than his master." If they persecuted me, they will persecute you also. If they obeyed my teaching, they will obey yours also. They will treat you this way because of my name, for they do not know the One who sent me. (John 15:20–21)

In fact, everyone who wants to live a godly life in Christ Jesus will be persecuted, while evil men and impostors will go from bad to worse, deceiving and being deceived. But as for you, continue in what you have learned and have become convinced of, because you know those from whom you learned it, and how from infancy you have known the holy Scriptures, which are able to make you wise for salvation through faith in Christ Jesus. (2 Timothy 3:12–15)

If the world hates you, keep in mind that it hated me first. If you belonged to the world, it would love you as its own. As it is, you do not belong to the world, but I have chosen you out of the world. That is why the world hates you. (John 15:18–19)

Teaching Your Daughter about Lordship

If the Most Important Thing You Can Do as a Parent Is Ground Your Daughter in Solid Christianity, Make Sure She Understands It!

"I believe in the Bible," Megan says during a class discussion. "I just don't believe *all* of it."

"Yeah. And I believe in God—you know, like a higher power that helps us and stuff," adds Nicole. "I just don't get into all that *Christianity* stands for."

You're probably hoping your daughter, Natalie—who *is* a Christian—will chime in and take a stand. In fact, if you could be on the sidelines watching her, you'd want to toss her some great arguments. Stuff like:

- Just *believing* there's a God isn't enough. Even Satan believes in God!

- Picking and choosing what we *will* and *won't* accept from the Bible is dangerous. It would be like choosing which laws of our country we don't like and simply disregarding them. Sooner or later, it'll catch up with us.

- There *is* an absolute truth. It's Jesus Christ and His Word.

You're the Coach

Well, in a sense, you *are* standing on the sidelines. No, you're not able to hear and see all your daughter's discussions in class or in the lunchroom, but as parents, you're the most important coach she'll ever have.

"I wish my mom would quit asking how much I weigh."

Vanessa, fourteen

Now is your opportunity not only to help her become grounded in a personal relationship with Christ but to help her understand it. Why is that so important? Because when we understand something, we can articulate it. And when we can verbalize our faith, we're not as likely to sit in the middle or to be lukewarm.

Chances are, you probably take your daughter to church, assume that she reads her Bible, and are proud that she professes to be a Christian. But there's a difference between *professing* Jesus as Lord and *understanding* what lordship is all about.

Breaking It Down

I imagine you pray often for your daughter. Are you also praying *with* her? As you make the time to pray together, read the Bible together, and discuss scripture together, you can unfold what lordship truly means.

Here are some suggested scriptures and specifics you can read and discuss together that will help your daughter gain a clearer perspective on making Jesus Lord of her life.

Lordship is . . .

Accepting the sovereignty of God. Take a peek at the leper's attitude in Matthew 8:2. He recognized the fact that Christ is in absolute control of our lives. Supreme control. He is the owner. The center of all. Everything belongs to Him. We are His subjects serving Him out of love for what He's done for us.

Help your daughter recognize this as fact. When Jesus truly becomes Lord of our lives, we give up our rights. All great men and women of God through the centuries first settled this issue. All that we own is His—our personality, possessions, faults, and talents.

Placing God first in every area of your life. Check out the discussion in Matthew 22:36–40. Is this a trick question? Someone's asking Jesus what the greatest commandment is. No trick. He responds that it's loving God with all of your heart, soul, and mind. In other words, He desires to saturate you. He wants the driver's seat. Lordship means allowing Him total reign.

Ask your daughter which areas of her life are easy to give God control of and which areas are struggle points. If we don't trust God *in* all and *with* all . . . we might as well say that we really don't trust Him *at* all.

Accepting responsibility and accountability. Recap the story found in Matthew 25:14. A wealthy man gives his servants control of specific divisions of money while he's away. What do they do? Two of them work hard and make wise investments; the other sluffs off, doesn't take his responsibility seriously, and sits on the money.

We are all held responsible for what God has entrusted to us. Remind your daughter of specific skills, talents, and responsibilities that God is entrusting to *her*. How is she handling the responsibility? Does she know that God holds her accountable? Are *you* holding her accountable?

Living in Lordship

As your daughter begins to understand and to live out the lordship of Jesus Christ, an exciting thing begins to happen—she takes ownership of her faith. And *that*, Mom, is your number-one goal, right? To know with absolute certainty that your daughter has a growing relationship with God, that she can verbalize her faith, and that she's understanding and owning His lordship.

Classroom Debates

Hey, Di!

I hate it! We're always getting into these debates in speech class and advanced biology. I know what I believe. . . . I just can't seem to articulate it very well.

Like I just don't buy this whole evolution theory. Why does Mrs. Owens keep presenting it like it's fact? It is still theory, right? And if she has a right to present her theories, don't I have a right to express mine?

I mean, like, I'd totally love to stand up and refute all that stuff, but I get so tongue-tied. And I don't really know what to say. All I know is that I don't buy it.

Sigh.

I'M TOTALLY FRUSTRATED!

Later.

Dear Di:

   I feel so stupid. I tried to take a stand against evolution in class today, but I just stammered around and didn't really say anything. I'm starting to feel sick to my stomach every time I walk into class. I want to share my beliefs, but I don't know how. It's like I'm missing an entire language or something.

   I hate this!

   I don't agree with anything that Mrs. Owens is saying . . . but I feel paralyzed.

   And I can feel my face turning red when she looks at me. She knows I disagree with her, but she also knows I don't have an argument to stand on.

Ugh!

What ARE the Facts?

In order for your daughter to hold her own in the classroom, she needs to know the facts. Let's take a peek at some of the most popular debates surging through classrooms today. Since creation versus evolution seems to be the most controversial and most talked-about issue in classrooms right now, let's begin—and spend a little more time—with this particular topic.

Creation versus Evolution

This has been hot for several years, and it'll continue to be popular for several more! You're probably aware of the controversy surrounding the state of Kansas since it mandated that if teachers present evolution in the classroom, they must also present the possibility of the creation theory.

Let's go over some basics, so you can help your daughter understand her arguments.

Of course, the entire debate begins with Darwin's theory that man evolved from animal over a series of time. And right here at the beginning is where you can help your daughter understand some fundamental differences within this argument.

Microevolution versus Macroevolution

Microevolution (horizontal) and macroevolution (vertical) are two completely different occurrences. While some moths and fruit flies have adapted to their environment with positive genetic adaptations, there has *never* been a *vertical* genetic mutation observed in real life or in fossil records.

The adaptive fruit fly remained the fruit fly. The adaptive peppered moth remained the peppered moth. There is simply no laboratory proof *or* paleontological proof that a lower life form has evolved up the scale of complexity into a more complex life form.

Scientist Arthur Koestler said, "In the meantime, the educated public continues to believe that Darwin has provided all the relevant answers by the magic formula of random mutations plus natural selection—quite unaware of the fact that *random mutations turned out to be irrelevant* and natural selection a tautology."[1]

So your daughter can begin with, "If man *did* go through some evolution processes, he's still going to be man. There's absolutely no proof available that man could ever have evolved from an entirely different life form, such as an ape."

And when her teacher shoots her down and continues, she can stand and ask, "And what, specifically, do you have as proof of that theory?"

Your daughter can continue with quotes from scientists Dr. Stephen J. Gould and Dr. Mark Ridley. Dr. Gould says: "All paleontologists know that the fossil record contains precious little in the way of intermediate forms. . . . Indeed our inability, even in our imagination, to construct functional intermediates in many cases, has been a persistent and nagging problem for gradualistic accounts of evolution."[2]

> "My mom gets her feelings hurt very easily. She compares our relationship to other mother/daughter relationships, and she tells me I don't love her. It really hurts."
>
> Zoe, seventeen

And Dr. Ridley states: "In any case, no real evolutionist, whether gradualist or punctuationist, uses the fossil record as evidence in favor of the theory of evolution as opposed to special creation."[3]

Statistics Discounting Evolution

Need more arguments? Dr. Carl Sagan estimates that the chance of life evolving on earth is one to $10^{2,000,000,000}$ (that is ten followed by two billion zeros!).

Just how big *is* this figure? Well, let's look at it this way: It would take six thousand books of three hundred pages each just to write the number!

This is approximately the same ridiculous probability that an entire high-school gym filled with dice could instantly explode and every one of the dice land on the number one!

I think it takes a lot more faith to believe man evolved from an ape than it does simply to believe we were created by a loving and powerful God.

Remember our former United States Surgeon General Everett Koop? Listen to what he says: "When I make an incision with my scalpel, I see organs of such intricacy that there simply hasn't been enough time for natural evolutionary processes to have developed them."[4]

Need a few more arguments? Your daughter can ask her teacher if he or she is willing to believe that the following simply happened by chance.

Facts about the Cosmos:
- The universe has one hundred billion galaxies.

- The Milky Way galaxy has one hundred billion stars. (If the earth and sun were one inch apart, you'd have to travel twenty-five thousand miles to reach the center of our galaxy.)

- The earth rotates on its axis at 1,000 mph.

- The earth moves around the sun at 70,000 mph.

- The solar system moves through space at 600,000 mph.

- The moon is 240,000 miles from the earth. (If the moon were one-fifth closer to earth, the tides would cover almost all land masses by thirty-five to fifty feet two times a day.)

Facts about the Human Body:
- The human body has one hundred trillion cells. (All the cells in the human body lined up side-by side-would encircle the earth two hundred times.)

- If all DNA in a human were placed end-to-end, it would reach the sun and back four hundred times.

- The human eye can handle 1.5 million simultaneous messages.

- In a day, the eye moves one hundred thousand times. (The body would have to walk fifty miles to exercise the leg muscles at an equal amount.)

- One hundred and thirty-seven million nerve endings pick up every message the eye sends to the brain.

- The inner ear contains as many circuits as the telephone system of a good-sized city.

- The human heart beats forty million times a year.

- All veins, arteries, and capillaries lined end-to-end would travel eighty thousand miles.

- A machine matching the human brain in memory capacity would consume electrical energy equivalent to one billion watts—half of the output of the Grand Coulee Dam. It would cost ten billion dollars, and it would fill the Empire State Building.

To suppose all this could have been formed by natural selection is . . . well . . . absurd!

Biblical Arguments against Evolution

Discuss *this* with your daughter!

Her teacher might say: "The six 'days' of creation are really six 'ages' or long periods of time."

Her response? Genesis 1:5 refers to a twenty-four-hour day (in Hebrew, *yom*) because of the accompanying terms *morning* and *evening*.

Genesis 1:5, 8, 17, 19, 23, and 31 are also concerned with the twenty-four-hour day because the terms *yom 1*, *yom 2*, *yom 3*, etc., always refer to a twenty-four-hour day in Scripture when accompanied by a numeral.

The Hebrew word *yamim* (plural for *yom*) appears more than seven hundred times in the Old Testament. When used in a historical context (as in Genesis 1), it always refers to literal twenty-four-hour days.

Let's check out how the Bible specifically describes creation: "For in six days the LORD made the heavens and the earth, the sea, and all that is in them, but he rested on the seventh day. Therefore the LORD blessed the Sabbath day and made it holy" (Exodus 20:11).

The context of the six days of creation and one day of rest is unmistakably a twenty-four-hour, seven-day week. "The Israelites are to observe the Sabbath, celebrating it for the generations to come as a lasting covenant. It will be a sign between me and the Israelites forever, for in six days the LORD made the heavens and the earth, and on the seventh day he abstained from work and rested" (Exodus 31:16–17).

The Hebrews used the term *yom rab* for "long time" and the term *olam* for "age." Genesis 1 and 2 use only the term *yom*, and it's used fourteen times.

The *order* of events in Genesis 1 would be impossible if *day* meant hundreds of millions of years! On day three, God made *mature* fruit trees with ripe fruit and all kinds of mature flowers with seeds to reproduce. There were no bees to pollinate the flow- ers—they came on day five. There was no sun to perform photo- synthesis—that came on day four. When God says He created the earth in six days, He did exactly that!

Abortion

A hot debate topic in thousands of speech and biology classes across America, the arguments for pro-choice are well-known and oftentimes delivered with venom. How can your daughter respond? Again, by knowing the facts. Here's how you can prepare her.

Common Arguments and Useful Responses

Pro-choice argument: The fetus is simply part of a woman's body—like her appendix, her teeth, or her gall bladder.

Pro-life response: No, it's really not. A body part is defined by the common genetic code it shares with the rest of its body. The genetic code of the unborn fetus is different than the mother's. How else would we explain that a mother is female yet can give birth to a male?

Pro-choice argument: A fetus is simply a blob of tissue. It's not really a human being.

Pro-life response: Hmmm. Is a blob of tissue able to develop its own heart? And by the way, that heart is actually beating at just six weeks after conception. At twelve weeks, eyes and hands are developed. And when did something "nonhuman" *become* human just by getting bigger?

Pro-choice argument: It's ridiculous—cruel even—to bring an unwanted child into the world.

Pro-life response: Maybe *pregnancies* are unwanted, but there are no unwanted children. Thousands of people are waiting in line to adopt . . . and yes, there *are* people willing to adopt a handicapped baby.

Pro-choice argument: It's not fair to a woman who was raped to have to give birth.

Pro-life response: First of all, it's extremely rare that a woman becomes pregnant through rape—her body is in a state of shock. But it *does* happen. And no, it wasn't fair. But since when do two wrongs make a right? It's just as unfair to end the life of the child who never asked to be born. Again, someone will adopt that child.

Pro-choice argument: If abortion becomes illegal, thousands of women will die from back-street procedures.

Pro-life response: Women are dying from *legal* abortions! Besides that . . . before abortion was legalized, only 10 percent of them were being done on the streets. That means 90 percent were still being done in physicians offices!

Biblical Arguments against Abortion

Your daughter can present the following verses to support the fact that God loves the unborn child.

Did not he who made me in the womb make them? (Job 31:15)

Before I formed you in the womb I knew you. (Jeremiah 1:5)

As soon as the sound of your greeting reached my ears, the baby in my womb leaped for you. (Luke 1:44)

For you created my inmost being; you knit me together in my mother's womb. (Psalm 139:13)

I like what my boss, Dr. James Dobson, says: "It's interesting to note . . . that a woman who plans to terminate a pregnancy usually refers to the life within her as 'the fetus.' But if she intends to deliver and love and care for the little child, she affectionately calls him 'my baby.' The need for this distinction is obvious: If we are going to kill a human being without experiencing guilt, we must first strip it of worth and dignity. We must give it a clinical name that denies its personhood."

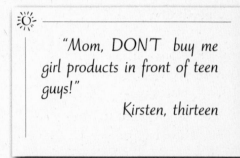

"Mom, DON'T buy me girl products in front of teen guys!"

Kirsten, thirteen

Gay Rights

How will your daughter respond to arguments that homosexuals should have special rights? Discuss the following arguments and responses with her.

Giving the Gay Community Minority Status

Argument: Homosexuals are being discriminated against. They deserve protected class status.

Response: Let's start by talking about what discrimination really is. African Americans have a history of being discriminated against. The gay community may be *criticized*—as are also the Christian community, mothers who breast-feed their babies on the job, citizens who believe in gun control, citizens who are against gun control, and TV evangelists—but no, they're not discriminated against. There's a big difference! How, specifically, are they being discriminated against?

Argument: Homosexuals suffer constant harassment because of their sexual orientation.

Response: While no one should be verbally or physically abused, the solution is not found in granting a minority status or protected class status to the gay community. That's like saying blondes should have a protected class status because people are always calling them "dumb blondes." Should left-handed people also receive protected class status? The real solution to verbal and physical abuse and sexual harassment is simply to use the laws that are already in effect.

Argument: Homosexuals are discriminated against all the time. For instance, they can't rent a certain apartment or buy the house they want because of their sexuality.

Response: Really? I'd like to see documentation on that. Homosexuals—like any other citizens—have the right to purchase or rent housing of their choice regardless of sexual orientation. Again, you're using the term *discrimination*, but you're not using it correctly. Let me give you some examples: Have homosexuals ever been denied the right to vote? Have they ever experienced legal segregation? Have public laws ever denied them access to specific drinking fountains, restrooms, or restaurants? Is the gay community living in a ghetto due to suffering economic hardship as a class because of discrimination? No. *That* would be discrimination.

Other Facets of the Homosexual Debate

Argument: It's perfectly normal to teach homosexuality as an alternative lifestyle to teenagers. After all, homosexuals were born that way—just as heterosexuals were born heterosexuals.

Response: What proof do you have that people are born homosexual? I'm not aware that that's ever been proven. If we teach homosexuality as an alternative lifestyle, then why not offer bestiality and pedophilia as viable alternative lifestyles and practices as well?

Argument: Homosexuals will say, "I've been this way since I can remember." That proves they were born homosexual.

Response: As long as I can remember, I've lived in the house on 34 Central Avenue. But that doesn't mean I was born there!

When someone says, "I've been this way since I can remember," it means exactly that—as long as he can remember. That doesn't include being born. No one can remember his birth. What's really meant by that statement is that they've felt different or experienced different feelings for as long as they can remember. This doesn't automatically make some-

> *"I wish my mom would let me wear what I want for picture day."*
>
> Natasha, twelve

one homosexual. He could be describing years in his childhood in which he felt alone, rejected, made fun of, or alienated by people who should have loved him. Again, none of these feelings make him homosexual. A homosexual lifestyle is a choice.

Argument: Homosexuality is not a choice. People wouldn't simply choose to be attracted to the same sex.

Response: All children need to be loved by two parents—a male and a female. Unfortunately, this isn't the norm in our society anymore. When a little boy doesn't receive the affection, attention, and love from an adult male figure that he so desperately needs, he'll grow up still yearning for that. It's going to be easy for him to transfer that normal desire for a healthy male role model into thinking, *Why am I yearning for male attention and acceptance? I must be homosexual.* This is a lie straight from Satan—who loves to confuse and deceive.

Euthanasia

With the news regarding Dr. Jack Kevorkian's jailing, assisted suicide is a hot topic for many folks right now. Do you know how your daughter feels about it? Does she know what it is? Does she understand the ramifications? Go through the following arguments with her, so she'll be able to stand her own in the classroom debate scene.

Argument: People shouldn't have to continue living without the quality of life they're used to having. It would be better to assist them in dying.

Response: What about someone who loses his job? His quality of life will drastically change as well. He won't be able to afford cable TV, the car he once drove, or the restaurants at which he used to eat. Should we help him die too?

Argument: To help someone who is suffering in pain to die is the most caring thing we can do.

Response: Killing isn't caring. It might seem merciful, or even compassionate, but it is *not* caring. Caring requires action, commitment, sacrifice, and personal involvement. Euthanasia is the exact opposite. Instead of investing time and energy into giving attention and care for that person, we use an alternative that promises to be swift and painless.

Argument: As long as we've created ways to help people die painlessly, we ought to practice those methods with those who wish it for themselves.

Response: This dependence on our own human knowledge and technology goes against what our Creator desires. In Proverbs 3:5–6, we are told to depend on God and God alone—not on science.

Argument: The patient certainly ought to have the right to end his own life if he so desires.

Response: Who, ultimately, owns the rights to life and death? The Bible tells us we have been bought with a great price—the blood of Christ. He created us, He died for us, and He owns us. God, and God alone, has the right to decide who will live and who will die—and when.

Argument: If a patient is only a limited time away from death anyway, he should have the right to decide how he will die. In this case, it would be permissible for him to have a professionally assisted suicide, so he can control his own death . . . instead of simply waiting to die.

Response: Even then he's not really in control of his death. Dr. Jack

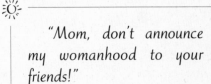

"Mom, don't announce my womanhood to your friends!"

Valerie, twelve

Kevorkian—when involved in assisted suicides—decided everything from which patients would be assisted, to the methods he would use, to the setting and timing of the deaths, and even the disposal of the bodies. This shows that the control still remains in the hands of the doctor—not the patient. Again, we don't have the right to demand our death. Only God does.

No one really knows if an assisted suicide is voluntary. Though earlier the patient may have stated that he wants to die, who knows at the very last millisecond what's going through his mind? What if, in the blink of an eye, he changes his mind? No one is able to know this, and yet he dies.

Wrapping It Up

Mom, allowing your daughter to go through her teen years not understanding why she believes what she does is like sending her to the wolves. If she doesn't learn to articulate her beliefs and take ownership of them, it's very likely that during her college years (or shortly after), she'll slowly begin to accept the world-view around her.

> *"I hate it when I'm really upset about something, and Mom just tells me my attitude is wrong. I wish she'd be more sympathetic and listen for a while then try to give me advice."*
>
> Carley, eighteen

Get into a good habit of talking through controversial topics with your daughter. Challenge her to think past the surface. When you ask her about her beliefs, don't allow her to settle for flimsy answers such as, "Well, I don't know" or "Just because." Keep pushing her thinking buttons. You're preparing her for battle. Make sure she's well equipped![5]

Father, I don't want my daughter to accept things blindly without thinking. Teach me how to motivate her to sift through the rumors and the facts and to accept only what is truth.

Help me to instill within her a thirst for knowledge. I confess, Father, that oftentimes I'm so tired when I get home, the last thing I want to do is have an engaging discussion on a controversial subject.

Strengthen me, Lord. Help me to stay current on events and world news so I can spark in my daughter that cutting-edge interest in our surroundings.

Amen.

☼ Memorize It . . . with Your Daughter ☼

When I called, you answered me; you made me bold and stouthearted. (Psalm 138:3)

Timothy, my son, I give you this instruction in keeping with the prophecies once made about you, so that by following them you may fight the good fight, holding on to faith and a good conscience. Some have rejected these and so have shipwrecked their faith. (1 Timothy 1:18–19)

For God did not give us a spirit of timidity, but a spirit of power, of love and of self-discipline. (2 Timothy 1:7)

Don't let anyone look down on you because you are young, but set an example for the believers in speech, in life, in love, in faith and in purity. (1 Timothy 4:12)

Handling the Cash

*Want Your Daughter to Handle Her Money Wisely
as an Adult? It Starts Now!*

Courtney just bought a brand-new pair of designer jeans for $64.99. Meredith is proud of her $89 athletic shoes. And Julia excitedly shows off her ski sweater she purchased for $58. So when your daughter wants a pair of boots that cost $72, she can't understand why you won't shell out the bucks.

"But all my friends get to buy what *they* want," she says. "Why can't I have the boots? I need them."

And she has a point—she *does* need a pair of boots. You gently explain, however, that you don't feel it's necessary to spend quite that much on something she'll outgrow in a year. "I'll take you shopping this Saturday, and we'll look for a more economical pair," you suggest.

Nope. That won't do. Everyone will know they're not the latest name brand. The next half-hour is spent in a discussion you'd rather forget.

Starting Now

Helping your daughter learn the value of money and how to budget and spend wisely is an important lesson that needs to begin early in life if you want those values carried into her adult years. If you haven't begun "money lessons" with her, consider starting now.

I'm fortunate that both my parents have always been good at managing money. They were both schoolteachers—Mom taught first grade, and Dad chaired the business division in a small Christian college. Both being in education, we never had a *lot* of money, but we always had enough. I realized later, it was because Mom and Dad knew how to spend and save wisely.

Dad taught courses in personal finance, and his major lesson to his students *and* his family was: Every time you get paid, tithe 10 percent and save 10 percent. His philosophy was if we put God first and always saved a little, we'd usually have enough to pay bills and do something extra.

> *"I hate being nagged as soon as I walk in the door about what I need to do. Let me unwind first!"*
>
> Velvet, fifteen

He was right. I'm so glad I learned that lesson early in life. And really—if we call ourselves Christians—tithing is non-negotiable. Christ should *always* be first, shouldn't He? If we call Him "Lord," shouldn't that affect our finances as well as the rest of our lives? Total surrender applies to every intricate detail of our lifestyle.

Passing It On

So how can you begin teaching your daughter about money *now*?

Allowance

Allowance is a great way to teach your daughter how to manage her own money. You might establish specific responsibilities you want her to accomplish for the allowance you give her. This weekly or monthly allotment may be for spending money, or it could be all-inclusive. For instance, I have a friend who gives her teen daughter a monthly allowance that has to include everything except school lunches. If she wants a new pair of shoes, she has to budget for them out of her monthly allotment. She wants to grab a pizza with friends Sunday night after church? It comes out of her allowance. In other words, it's up to *her* to decide how she'll spend her money, but when it's gone, it's gone.

This is an excellent way to teach the value of money. If she has to do without pizza and movies for two months to purchase the seventy-two dollar pair of designer boots, she may think twice and eventually learn to settle for a more reasonably priced pair.

Bank Accounts

Consider helping your daughter open her own checking and saving accounts, and teach her how to balance her books. This will not only give her immediate ownership of her money, it will also show her that how she handles it has direct consequences.

Biblical Application

Spend time guiding your daughter through specific scriptures that talk about money. Here are some suggested questions to discuss as you search the Bible together.

- Why did Jesus say the poor woman who gave her last few cents actually gave more than the wealthy folks who dropped *several dollars* into the offering?

- Why was the wealthy master angry at one of his three servants who simply buried his money instead of investing it as the other two did? Is he against saving money?

- What specifically does Jesus say about stewardship?

- Why is tithing important?

- Can we be all that God calls us to be *without* tithing?

Shuffling the Bucks

When it comes to handling money, you want your daughter adopting *your* views and practices—not the world's. This is one time you *don't* want to "pass the buck." Invest in your daughter's life by *showing* her how to tithe, budget, spend, and save wisely.

Though my family never had a lot of money, we always took a summer vacation, we always had wonderful holidays, and we always had new school clothes. Why? Because Mom and Dad knew how to make wise financial decisions with the little they had.

The bottom line? Jesus was always first at our house. Mom and Dad would never have *considered* skipping their tithe even one month for something else. I believe God rewards that kind of faithfulness. By practicing good stewardship, we're showing God by our actions that we trust Him to meet our needs. And you know what? He does. And He will.

Stewardship is a big deal to God. Did you know that stewardship is mentioned in one-third of all the parables Jesus gives throughout the Bible? Teach your daughter *now* that tithing and putting God first in our finances is a privilege. He actually owns everything we have, right? It's an honor to be able to give Him back at least 10 percent of what we receive.

Sexual Purity

Dear Diary:

Sometimes I feel like I'm the only teenage girl in the world who's a virgin! Katie and Derek have only been dating two weeks, and they've already done it.

And Aimee's always bragging about her weekends with Dustin.

But you know who's really getting to me? Kiley.

I don't get it.

She comes to youth group and church and Bible study. And she says she's a Christian. But today she told me that she and Evan are having a lot of fun . . . sexually.

And I'm all, "But Kiley! You know sex outside of marriage is wrong."

And she's all, "Duh. I didn't say we're having sex sex. I said we're having a lot of fun . . . sexually."

Anyway, she finally spilled it out: She says they're having oral sex. And that since it's not sexual intercourse, it's okay.

Hey . . . sex is sex.

Isn't it?

Diary, I'm confused.

What Is Sexual Purity?

As Christian adults we have proclaimed "Be a virgin!" to our children so much over the past few years that we have forgotten an essential component in that declaration—and that's the fact that sexual purity and virginity are not one in the same.

Moms, we have a great battle on our hands! I hear from Christian teen girls all across the nation who believe that as long as they're not engaged in sexual intercourse, they're sexually pure. Take a quick peek at what some of our Christian girls are thinking.

Dear Susie:

Conner and I have been dating for three months. We're both Christians and have been saving sex until marriage. He says everything else, though, is okay.

At first I was unsure, but we really do love each other. And our physical involvement has truly brought us closer together. I've never felt as close to anyone in my whole life as I do to Conner! He's terrific.

Last night at youth group, we had a special speaker talk about sexual purity. I don't know . . . it got me to thinking. I'm starting to have a few doubts about what Conner and I are doing . . . and if it's really okay. He still says we're fine. I mean, after all, we pray at the end of every date.

We're not having sex. We're just doing a lot of touching and petting and putting our hands everywhere. Know what I mean? We're still virgins, so we're both still sexually pure, right?

Curious,
Medford, Oregon

I wish I could personally take this girl out to lunch, sit across from her, and discuss what sexual purity really is. I'd also love to chat with her mom . . . whom I'm assuming has no idea that her daughter is so physically involved with her boyfriend. After all, they're both good teens, right? They're involved in church, and they probably never break curfew, drink, or smoke. Yet they both have a very false picture of sexual purity.

Mom, have you discussed sexual purity with your daughter? I mean *really* discussed it? Does she know the difference between sexual purity and virginity, or does she assume they're the same thing?

Where does your daughter stand on sexual purity? Where do *you* stand on sexual purity? Is it an important enough issue for you to make sure—beyond all conceivable doubt—that your daughter knows what God intends and what you as her mom intend for her?

"One of my favorite things to do with my mom is walk together. This way we both get our exercise, and we get to talk with each other without anyone else around."
Hannah, eighteen

Let's Get It Straight

If you haven't already, please set the record straight: Anyone can say no to having sexual intercourse. That doesn't mean she's living a sexually pure life. The girl in the above letter is a virgin, but she's not sexually pure.

Thousands of Christian teens are walking down the aisle on their wedding day proclaiming virginity and *thinking* they've maintained sexual purity until marriage, but they've been deceived.

Let's hear what another girl has to say:

Dear Susie:

When I was in the seventh grade, our youth group had a special "True Love Waits" evening. I made a commitment to wait until I'm married before having sex. A lot of other kids in my youth group made the same commitment.

When I was a junior in high school, I began dating a guy from another church across town. He talked about God and seemed like a really cool guy. We started kissing after the second date. By the fifth time we went out, he was getting really handsy. When I hesitated or started to pull back, he would say, "I'm a Christian. I'm totally into not having sex till marriage. You don't have anything to worry about."

Well, I really liked him, so I kind of let myself go and trusted him. Over time, we got more and more intimate, until we were finally undressing each other. We still weren't having sex, though. And he'd always bring up how important it was to wait and only have sex with our future spouses.

After we had dated for eight and a half months, we started having oral sex. He convinced me it was okay because we weren't having intercourse. "This is how we get around the whole premarital sex thing," he said. He kept saying it was okay to have fun and get fulfilled sexually, as long as we didn't have intercourse—and that as long as we maintained our virginity we were still in God's will.

We broke up three years ago, and I'm still feeling guilty about everything we did. I know this: I don't want to experience any sexual fulfillment outside of marriage. I want to have the whole thing with my future husband. And that's what I'm totally committed to now.

But my question is, how come no one talks about how wrong getting so physical is? I've asked God to forgive me, and now that I'm out of the relationship, I can clearly see that what we did was sinful. But you know what? I have lots of friends in college who are just as physically involved as I used to be, and they're saying it's okay and they're still sexually pure.

What's going on? It's really not okay . . . is it?

Cheyenne, Wyoming

Wow. My heart breaks for the girl who is deceived into thinking that simply because she's not involved in intercourse, she can do everything else that gives her or her boyfriend pleasure. When God tells us to stay sexually pure until marriage, He's not talking about a specific *act* as much as He is a *lifestyle*.

Sexual purity involves everything we put into our minds and our ears. Can we look at soft porn and be sexually pure? No. Can we watch sexual acts in movies and television

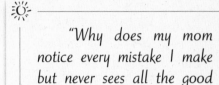

"Why does my mom notice every mistake I make but never sees all the good stuff?"

Tiffany, fourteen

and claim to be sexually pure? No. The Bible tells us to guard our hearts very carefully. God knows that whatever we dwell on will eventually take up residence in our lives.

If you disagree with that, then I'm assuming you also disagree with "I can watch violent movies, play violent video games, and make bombs in my garage without actually living or acting it out." Come on, moms! Wake up!

Be a Mirror

If your daughter sees you absorbed in soap operas and movies filled with sexual themes, she's going to assume it's okay for her too. And even if you tell her it's *not* permissible for her at this time, she'll get the message that when she's older it *is* permissible . . . because she sees *you* doing it.

Moms, *you* are the greatest Bible your daughter will ever read. How are your pages being reflected? Do you allow questionable videos to be brought inside your home? Do you know what your daughter is watching and listening to when she's at the home of a friend? Are you setting the godly example that God needs you to set for your daughter?

I've created an inside peek at what very likely is going on in your daughter's mind if she's confused about the difference between sexual purity and abstinence. I'll set this up as a conversation between God and a teen girl, okay? This will help you understand how easy it is for a girl—possibly your daughter—to rationalize God's standard of purity. After reading it, will you share it with your daughter? It will make a great discussion!

God Said . . . I Said

I said: Where's that CD?

God said: Next to your jeans.

I just saw it two days ago.

Underneath your university sweatshirt.

Never can find anything when I need it.

On top of the pillow on your bed.

Ugh!

You're ignoring Me.

I'll bet Lacey took it.

Listen to Me.

She's always sneaking into my room and borrowing my stuff!

I'm talking to you.

Kid sisters!

If you'll stop long enough to listen, you'll hear Me.

Lacey!

I'm waiting.

My chemistry book. Notebook. Backpack. Hair clips. Purple nail polish. Pillow.

Jeans.

Jeans.

University sweatshirt.

University sweatshirt.

CD.

Ah! Here it is!

Now that you've got what you want, how 'bout listening to Me for a few minutes?

Hey, there's my student Bible. Sheesh! Haven't seen *that* in a while. In fact . . . wow. I haven't picked this up since . . . well, since Jarod and I started dating. Whew, this is dusty! Oh yeah, here's my bookmark from camp. Wow, what a week *that* was! God was so close then.

And I'm yearning to be close again.

But He seems so far away now.

I'm as close as your heart.

And I don't really *feel* Him anymore.

You don't really *pray* anymore.

Sigh. Seems like forever since we've talked.

Yes. Think about it. Why have you stopped talking with Me?

Ah . . . those camp days. Everything seemed so simple then.

Jarod wasn't in the picture.

But since Jarod and I started dating . . . I don't know. It's like I'm not as free to talk about stuff with God like I used to.

Think about it. Come on.

Ah, what am I doing sitting around reminiscing?

No, don't stop. I'm trying to get through.

It's just that . . . well . . . hey! Here's my memory verse—all highlighted in fluorescent yellow. James 4:28.

Yes! Come on. I'm *yearning* to be with you.

Wow. A lot sure has happened since camp. Well . . . a lot's happened since Jarod and I got together.

Keep on. You're getting close. Talk to Me.

Sigh. I miss the intimacy God and I used to have.

No. Not third person. It's Me! Direct your thoughts to Me—first person. Come on!

There was a time I couldn't wait to open the Bible and read His words.

You're getting closer . . . not *His* words . . . My words.

I told Him everything. Hey, what is this? Why am I getting so sappy? I found the CD I was looking for. Lacey didn't take it after all. I guess just flipping through my student Bible is bringing back so many memories. I don't know . . . I feel sad. Distanced. Alone.

You're never alone. I'm right here.

Sigh. Oh, God. What happened?

YES! Finally. We're talking. I love you, My child.

God?

Yes! It's Me.

God?!? I can't believe it. You're here!

I never left.

Why have You been so distant?

I haven't. I've been right here the whole time.

But I haven't felt close to you.

You haven't *been* close to Me.

But . . . You just said You never left.

I didn't. *You* did.

Well, Father, I . . . uh, I don't know.

Yes, you do.

Yeah. Okay. Well, I just haven't felt comfortable enough to talk with You. Something's changed.

Yes. Something *has* changed. Disobedience will do that. It places distance between us. Remember Adam and Eve? They tried to hide from Me. They disobeyed, and they felt distant because of it.

Is disobedience the only thing that causes distance?

No. Guilt will cause it too.

Guilt.

Guilt from disobedience.

I'm striking out, aren't I?

Talk to Me.

Well . . . uh . . . okay. So. Um . . . hey, this is weird. I don't know what to say. It's been too long.

It's never too long.

Well, I'm just not comfortable talking to You anymore.

I know. That's why we need to talk.

So how come You don't like Jarod?

I love Jarod. I *died* for him. In fact . . . if he were the only person in the entire world, I still would have gone to all the trouble to create it just as beautiful as it is.

Huh?

Think about it. The Grand Canyon. The Great Barrier Reef. Niagara Falls. Snow-capped mountains. Lush, green rain forests. Rolling hills. An indescribable sunset. Double rainbows. If Jarod were the only human being on this entire planet, I would not have shorted him at all. I would have given as much attention to detail—rhyme and color and the variety of species—just for him.

Wow.

Don't ever forget, My child, that I love him that much.

That's incredible, God!

And I love *you* that much too.

It doesn't feel like it.

Disobedience—

I know. I know. Disobedience will do that.

Right.

So it's not about Jarod?

Well, partly. But it's also about you. Each person must take responsibility for his own actions.

Yeah, I guess.

So . . . are you ready to talk?

Sigh. All right.

Go ahead.

I love him.

I'm listening.

And he loves me.

And?

So we love each other.

Go on.

Well, that's it.

No, it's not.

Well, how far are we going with this?

Let's talk about how far *you're* going.

I knew this was coming.

What do you want to tell Me?

I don't *want* to tell You anything. But since I *need* to . . . and since You already know . . . well, okay. Here it is: We're not having sex.

Go on.

That's enough, isn't it?

No. We need to talk it out.

This is really personal, God. I mean . . . this is intimate stuff.

My child, I *created* You. You can't get more intimate than that.

Well, yeah. But still . . . Jarod and I aren't having sex.

What are you having?

A good time. But it's not sex.

What *is* sex?

Well, You know. You created it, remember?

Yes, but I want to hear it from you.

Sex . . . is . . . well, it's . . . intercourse.

Intercourse.

Yeah. Intercourse.

That's it?

Intercourse. Sex is two people having intercourse.

Hmmm. I'd say it's a lot more than that.

Whaddya mean? How can sex be more than intercourse?

Sex is the uniting of two people in an intimate way.

Through intercourse.

It's two bodies intertwining together—physically, emotionally, and spiritually. Again, sex is way more than intercourse. You said it yourself: I invented sex.

Yeah?

So since I invented it, I ought to have a say in how and where it works best. And that's in marriage. My plan is for you to remain sexually pure until marriage.

But I am! I'm not having sex.

Correction: You're not having *intercourse*. But you are *not* living a sexually pure lifestyle.

How come? I'm a virgin!

You can technically be a virgin without being sexually pure.

What?

Thousands of young adults walk down a church aisle to be joined in marriage proclaiming their virginity. But guess what?

What?

I'm not as interested in your virginity as I am in your sexual purity.

But—

Anyone can say no to intercourse.

And I have!

But it takes a lot more than simply refraining from intercourse to be sexually pure.

So what are we talking about?

We're talking about you and Jarod.

We love each other.

You and Jarod have become one.

But how? We've never done it.

You've never had intercourse, but you *have* become intimately acquainted with each other's bodies.

But we've never—

You've been intimate.

No. We really haven't. . . .

Dishonesty. Disobedience. Remember the reasons you've felt so distant from Me?

Well, yeah. But, God, we never . . . I mean, we . . . uh . . .

It's just us. Come on. Be specific.

I don't. He never. I mean, I um—

You can be intimate with him yet have trouble just *talking* about it with Me?

No. Well, yeah. Hey, this is embarrassing.

Okay. I'll start. Again . . . you've been intimate with each other. Your hands have gone where they shouldn't. You've crossed boundaries that should be reserved only for marriage.

But we've never had sex!

Yes, you have. Sex is intimacy with someone of the opposite sex. You and Jarod have been intimate.

I . . . I . . .

Even though you've never had intercourse, you are NOT sexually pure.

Well, then I might as well have intercourse!

In My mind, you already have.

What?!?

It's in My Word—I've made it explicitly clear. If you even *look* at someone with lust in your heart, you've crossed a line I don't want you to cross.

So in Your mind . . . Jarod and I have had sex?

Have you been intimate with him?

Yes.

Did it ever cross your mind that this is what you'd like to be doing with your future husband?

Well, yeah.

You've allowed Jarod to experience something with you that should be shared only with your future husband.

But—

And in a sense, you've stolen from Jarod's future wife.

I don't get it.

You're giving him an intimacy that only she should experience with Jarod.

Well . . . why didn't You stop me?

I'll never treat you like a puppet. You'll always have free will. I'll never force you to obey My commands. But I *did* use My Holy Spirit to prick your conscience.

Is that why I was feeling guilty?

Yes.

And that's why I was feeling so far away from You?

Yes. Again . . . disobedience will do that.

But, God . . . we love each other.

Do you love *Me?*

Sure.

Pick it up.

What?

Your student Bible.

Yeah, here it is.

Flip over to John 14:21. What's it say?

It's pretty much saying that if I love You, I'll obey You. So, what are You saying? That I don't love You?

No, *you're* saying it . . . by your actions.

But God, I love You. Come on!

If you really love Me, you'll obey Me. You'll want to please Me. You'll allow Me to guide you . . . instead of Jarod . . . or your emotions.

Are you saying I've sinned?

That's exactly what I'm saying.

Well, in Your eyes, if I've already had sex, I might as well actually go ahead and do it!

Oh no, My child. There are always consequences.

What hope do I have?

You have all kinds of hope. I *am* hope!

I don't get it.

Forgiveness. It's yours for the asking.

Well, sure, for stuff like lying and cheating and saying bad words or watching a movie I shouldn't have seen. But *sex?*

Yes.

You'll forgive me for going too far physically?

Yes. If you *seek* forgiveness.

Okay. Will You forgive me?

Not yet.

What?!? You just said—

Repentance, My child. It's all about repentance.

But I *did* repent. I just asked You to forg—

True repentance means "I don't ever plan on going down that road again," NOT "I'll get forgiven now, and after Jarod and I make out tomorrow night, I'll get forgiven again."

Hey, how'd You know I was thinking that?

Whom are you talking to?

God. Right.

Repentance reflects the condition of your heart.

Well, my heart wants to be forgiven.

Not really.

Come on, God!

You're still not convinced you've actually sinned. You're sorry . . . but mainly sorry you're being called on it. You're sorry you've been "caught." You're sorry you've felt so distanced from Me. And you're sorry you haven't been praying or reading your Bible. But . . . you're not *really* sorry you've been intimate with Jarod.

Father, we love each other.

Do you want a lifetime of sexual fulfillment . . . or a night here and there of short-lived experiences?

Definitely a lifetime!

Do you want a partner . . . or a soul mate—a man who's as crazy about you when you reek with bad breath and a bed-head as he is when you're wearing that little red dress with the red shoes?

Wow. Bed-head. No makeup.

And when you're sick . . . head over the toilet battling the flu.

And stinky.

***That,* My child, is a soul mate. *That* is true love.**

I don't have that with Jarod.

No, you don't.

How come?

A couple of reasons: Jarod is basing your relationship on feelings, not commitment. You see, commitment is a *decision*. It overrides feelings.

I'm not sure I know what You mean.

If the commitment is there, what you look like—how much weight you gain through the years, a terminal illness you may suffer, the disfigurement you may receive from an auto accident—none of that will decrease the love factor between the two of you . . . because your love will be based on commitment, not feelings.

I guess feelings can be pretty fleeting, huh?

Exactly. Here today, gone tomorrow.

Wow. What Jarod and I have is special . . . but it's nowhere near *that* deep!

Let me ask you something.

K.

Ever heard of alopecia areata?

No.

It's a disease that affects thousands.

What is it?

It's an autoimmune deficiency. Your immune system thinks you're allergic to your own hair. So, basically . . . you start losing your hair.

You mean . . . go bald?

Right.

Is it men or women or both?

Both, but mostly women.

Old women?

No. Mostly young women—even children and teenagers.

Wow. I can't imagine.

Here's the question: If you contracted alopecia, would your relationship with Jarod change at all?

Are You kidding? Jarod *loves* my hair. He's always playing with it, smelling it, . . . well . . .

But why would your relationship change?

Well . . . because. I mean, I'd be lacking something. I wouldn't be all there. I mean . . . I *want* to say it wouldn't matter—it wouldn't matter at all. But—somehow deep inside—I'd be kidding myself. I *know* it would matter to him. Things would change.

How would your relationship change?

Well, it probably wouldn't take long for Jarod to find another healthy head of hair. I think he'd stick with me at the beginning—

You know, try to comfort me and all that. But . . .

But six or seven months later?

I don't like admitting this . . . but I really believe he'd move on.

Hmmm. What if you had to have a mastectomy?

At *my* age?

It would be extremely rare, but it *could* happen.

Oh, please, God. Don't even go there.

Think about it.

Okay, but only for a second.

Fair enough. Would this change in your outer appearance affect your relationship with Jarod?

Yeah, probably . . . eventually.

My child, these are real possibilities that can happen in a lifetime. But over the course of years, a marriage built on Me can withstand *any* obstacle.

Wow. I've never known a love like that.

I love you like that.

Yes, but You're GOD. I've never known human love like that.

That's because you've never been in an opposite-sex relationship that has been centered on Me.

Oh.

Which brings Me to the second reason.

Huh?

Remember, a few minutes ago? We were talking about being a soul mate with your future husband. You said that you and Jarod have never had that.

Oh, yeah. And I asked why.

And I said . . .

A couple of reasons. One is that our relationship is based on feelings instead of commitment—real commitment that can weather the storms of life changes and disease and everyday struggles.

Right.

And the second reason?

Your relationship is not centered on Me.

So, can we *get* it centered on You?

You've just told me that Jarod isn't your soul mate—that he probably *wouldn't* stay through the long haul if things became difficult. Why would you want to continue a relationship that's surface . . . temporary?

Because he's all I have!

Hmmm.

Oh, wow. Did I actually say that out loud?

Yes.

Oooh.

But even if you hadn't, I still would have heard your thoughts.

Oh, yeah.

My child, I long for you to trust *Me* with your love life.

But, God, I want someone who's—

Capable of making you feel secure? And cherished? A young man who's not afraid to cry with you? Someone who will spontaneously surprise you with a picnic lunch by the lake? Fly a kite with you on a windy day? Romance you? Bring you flowers? Someone who's strong. Deeply committed to Me. Involved in church. One who helps Widow Foster out of her car and up the steps to church on Sunday morning. A young man who stops in the hallway between Sunday school and morning worship to pick up a three year old and tousle his hair. Someone who makes you laugh and who treats you like a princess. Someone who's head-over-heels crazy about you and really doesn't care if your hair is long or short or if you had the extra helping of dessert you really didn't need. A man who's excited about providing for you. One who brings out the very best in you and enhances your relationship with Me.

I don't know what to say.

That's whom you're longing for . . . isn't it?

Oh, yes, Father. That's the cry of my heart! That's *exactly* the man I want to spend the rest of my life with!

Is Jarod that man?

You know he isn't.

Go on.

Jesus, he's nowhere near that description.

Then why are you dating him?

I . . . I . . . I *thought* we loved each other. But now . . . after all this . . . oooh. I hate admitting this, but I think I've been dating him . . . just to date him. You know. It felt good. I belonged to someone. And I like the attention. It feels good to be kissed and . . . well, You know.

Do you believe now that I know exactly the kind of man you want . . . you need?

Oh, yes! You hit the nail right on the head! You gave a *perfect* description of the man I want to marry.

Then trust Me.

I trust You.

Trust Me with your love life.

Oh, that.

Trust that in My perfect timing, I will bring exactly whom I want in your life.

But that may take awhile! I know Your timing, God. You're just not as fast as I wish You were.

But I'm never late.

But You *do* take awhile.

Will You trust Me?

Well . . . what if You forget me and—

There's only one thing I forget.

What's that?

Forgiven sins.

Smile.

Everything else is right at the forefront of my mind.

But . . . You're dealing with persecuted Christians in Sudan, and earthquakes in Turkey, and high-school shootings, and drug busts, and—

And your future.

You mean . . .

Your friends and your relationships are every bit as important to Me as disease and famine and all the other wrongs in the world.

No way.

Believe it. Everything that concerns you, concerns Me.

That's incredible. I don't deserve that kind of attention.

I *died* so you *could* have this kind of attention.

I'm so sorry, Father.

It's starting.

What?

Your heart is beginning to look like a repentant heart.

I think I'm finally beginning to understand.

I'm listening.

I don't want to steal from my future husband.

No.

I've been selfish. I've been with Jarod for what *I* could get out of the relationship. I mean, he made me feel special. He was someone to take me to homecoming and to go out with on weekends. And . . . well, the physical stuff . . . it felt good.

That's because I created you as a sexual being. It's *supposed* to feel good—but it's also supposed to be *saved* for one man.

The man you described?

Yes. The man who is My choice for your lifetime mate.

I feel sick to my stomach.

Oh?

Yeah. I'm so sorry I became involved with Jarod, Father. It all seems so stupid now! I mean . . . he's not the man You described. And if I know he's not the man I want and need in a soul mate, why am I messing around with him? You're right, God. I've cheated him. I have given him physically and emotionally what only his wife should.

Even though you didn't have intercourse?

Yeah. I see it now, God. Even though we didn't have intercourse, we were still bonded together. We felt as one—emotionally, physically. Oh . . . I am so sorry! I mean, I really am, Jesus. I am really, really sorry! I can't believe I rationalized all that. I actually talked myself into believing everything was fine—that what we were doing was permissible because we loved each other. But if real love is the way you described it—something that overrides feelings—Jarod and I are nowhere near that. We don't have real love, God. What we have . . . is . . . well . . . what *do* we have?

Lust.

Ouch.

You have a relationship based on physical attraction.

You make it sound so surface. And it *is* . . . I just . . . man! I'm ashamed, Father. I'm really sorry. This is not what I want. Not at all.

Now you're ready.

Ready? For what?

To seek forgiveness. You have a repentant heart.

Oh, God, I really do seek Your forgiveness. I don't *ever* plan to go down this road again. I want to save myself for my future husband. Will You forgive me, Father?

I forgive you.

And will You help me?

Yes. I forgive . . . and I forget. And I would *love* to help you, but I need you to do your part.

Anything, Father. What is it?

I need you to give Me total control of your love life.

And that means . . .

Let Me write your love story. Trust Me to bring the right man into your life. I want to relieve you of all that pressure.

But I still have to be on the lookout, right?

No. You don't have to do anything except be totally in love with Me.

You mean . . . I don't even have to *look* for him?

No. That's My job. *Your* job is to trust Me. Remember, I know you better than you even know yourself, because I created you. I know—even more than you do—what and who will fulfill you, make you happy, and draw you continually closer to Me. I know all that. Trust Me with it.

This sounds too good to be true.

Believe it.

I don't even have to *look* for him?

All you have to do . . . is be totally in love with Me.

How do I get more in love with You, Father?

How do you become more acquainted with *anyone*?

Hmmm. I spend time with him. Tell him stuff. Listen to him. We do things together.

Works the same way with Me.

Sounds easy.

Spend time with Me—the way you used to. Remember when you were looking for your CD and found your student Bible?

Yeah.

You were reminiscing about camp days and how close we were. There was a time you couldn't wait to tell Me everything. A time you longed to open My Word and read and grow.

Yeah! I want that again. I really want that again, Father.

I'm still in the same place. You're the one who moved, remember?

Yeah. I'm so sorry. Jesus, now that You've forgiven me, let's start over, okay? I'd really love to have a clean slate.

It's yours.

But I'm gonna need help.

That's what I'm here for.

I mean . . . right now it's all so clear. But I'm afraid when Jarod looks at me with those puppy-dog eyes, I'm gonna melt right into his hands.

I can give you the strength to call it off with Jarod.

I need to do that, don't I?

Yes. We've already established the fact that he's not the man I want you to spend the rest of your life with.

It's still going to be hard.

Yes, but you're not alone. And after you've ended your relationship with Jarod, I want to teach you about healthy, godly boundaries. I want to teach you how to live a sexually pure lifestyle.

Doesn't that just mean not going too far with the opposite sex?

No, it's a lot more than that. Sexual purity is a *lifestyle*.

What do You mean, Jesus?

It involves what you listen to and watch, how you act and react. It's establishing holy safeguards around your life—protecting yourself from the deceit of Satan.

Yeah, I'll need You to help me big-time with all that. We've got a lot of work to do, huh, Father?

And one more thing.

Yeah?

Trusting Me with your love life . . . means trusting Me *forever* with your love life.

I *think* I know what You mean.

Let's make sure.

Okay.

Remember . . . I want to establish a love life with you. I want you to be so in love with Me that your biggest concern is simply growing closer to Me.

I want that too, Jesus. And I'm going to spend time with You and continue to give You all of me, so we *can* have that kind of relationship.

What if I choose not to bring a man into your life?

What?

What if I choose not to share you with a man?

Oh, Jesus. You would do that?

My ways are not for you to know yet.

Oh, Father, You know my heart. You know my desires.

Yes, I created you.

I never thought that You might choose to keep me single.

What if I do?

A lifetime of being alone?

Not alone, My child. You are never alone.

I know.

What if I choose not to share you with a man?

I can't understand that, Jesus.

I know. But with My strength, you can accept *without understanding*.

Accept without understanding.

That's spiritual maturity.

In Your strength, I can accept without understanding.

In My strength . . . you can accept without understanding.

Wow.

Do you trust Me?

Yes, Jesus. I do.

Do you love Me?

Yes, Father. And I want to love You more.

Yes?

Yes! I want to fall in love with You more and more every single day of my life.

Yes!

Jesus, You know my heart. You created me. You know I yearn for a husband—the man You described earlier. I'm trusting You for him. But if . . . for reasons I'll never understand . . . You choose *not* to bring him into my life, I'm still going to trust You. It will *not* affect my relationship with You.

Yes!

I love You, Jesus. I really, really love You. *You*, Father, are the love of my life. And until You bring Your choice for a lifetime mate—or even if You don't—I'm simply going to concentrate on being in love with You.

I'm so proud of you, My child. I love you more than you'll ever comprehend.

But, God?

Yes?

What about my physical involvement with Jarod? I wish I'd never gone down that path.

Me too . . . but you're forgiven. In fact, I've already wiped your slate clean. It's forgotten.

I commit my sexual purity to You, Jesus.

Thank you. I'll give you the strength to *keep* that commitment.

I need to break if off with Jarod.

I'll go with you.

Thanks. I'll need all the help I can get.

I'll give you the words. I'll provide the strength.

I love You, Jesus! I love You!

And I love *you*, My child.

Let's Back Up

Of course, sexual purity doesn't happen in an instant. Hopefully, this is something you're already in the process of teaching your daughter. I *hope* it's been happening for years. When is the best time to teach sexual purity to your daughter? All her life—starting at the beginning!

What's the best way to *continue* the lesson? With your life—lived *consistently* in front of her and her friends.

You're probably aware of the True Love Waits movement. It actually began in the early '90s with Christian teenagers who pledged to save themselves until marriage. Literally millions of Christian teens have made—and still make—True Love Waits pledges.

"Listen when I'm telling you something. You know — look at me. Understand."

Meredith, seventeen

I have friends at church who decided to make this a special family night for their son and daughter. They purchased rings with the inscription "True Love Waits" and wrapped them as special gifts.

On a designated evening, the parents made dinner reservations at a classy restaurant, everyone dressed up, and away they went. The teens didn't have any idea what was going on. They simply thought they were being treated to a nice dinner by their parents.

After they had placed their dinner order, Jeff and Kathy began talking with their two children about sexual purity. Even though they'd had this discussion several times before, they simply wanted to reiterate the message. "This is what God intends for you," stated Jeff as he shared God's plan of perfect love within marriage.

"And this is what *we* expect of you," added Kathy as she emphasized rules of dating, boundaries, and guidelines.

As Matthew and Kelly reiterated their vows to maintain sexual purity until marriage, their parents pulled out the gift boxes containing the special rings.

"We want you to wear this ring as a reminder of the pledge you've made to remain sexually pure until you're married," Jeff said. "It's not just a promise made to your mother and me. This is a sacred oath you're making to God, to yourself, to your future mate, and to your future children."

"Every time you feel that ring against your skin," Kathy said, "let it be a reminder of this sacred oath you've made."

"And also know that we're supporting you in this pledge," Jeff continued. "Your mom and I will pray earnestly for you and will trust Christ to lead you in all your relationships."

That evening was a frozen moment for Kelly and Matthew. "I'll never forget it," Matt says. "There's no way I'll jeopardize my relationship with Christ or my parents' faith in me by getting sexually involved outside of marriage. I'm committed to purity. I want my wife to have *all* of me."

Your Daughter Needs Support

Have you taken the time to explain to your daughter the importance of not only abstinence but sexual purity? Consider planning a special evening for her like Jeff and Kathy did for their teens.

There are several different ways to present your daughter with a sexual purity covenant. When Cassie turned thirteen, her dad had flowers delivered to the house, the two of them got dressed up, and he took her on a date. "My wife and I decided that we wanted her first date to be with her dad," John explained. "So I went all out—flowers, suit and tie, the works."

He made reservations at a downtown restaurant and opened the car and restaurant doors for her all evening. "As I pulled her chair out from the table for her, I said, 'Cassie, someday you'll be dating, and this is how your date is supposed to treat you,'" John remembers. "I wanted her to expect nothing less than the very best behavior from her future dates, so I took care to help her set her standards high."

They talked throughout the evening about what kind of guy she'd like to marry some day, the most important qualities in a relationship, and the fact that Christ has to be the very center of all she does.

"It was a magical evening," Cassie says. "I truly felt like a princess. Then, to my surprise, over dessert my dad pulled out a black velvet box and handed it to me. I had no idea what was inside."

"When she opened the box to see the gold ring, I told her this was her mom's and my covenant to her—that we would hold her accountable with her relationships, pray for her, and always be available to talk with her," John says.

"It gives me so much strength and support to know my parents are in this thing with me," Cassie says. "They believe in me, plus they have high expectations of me. With God's strength, I won't let them down, I won't let my future husband down, and I'm not going to let myself down."

Interested?

Of course, you don't have to actually give a physical item such as a ring or necklace to your daughter to make a sexual purity covenant with her. The *pledge* is what's important. It's just as sacred of an oath with or without a piece of jewelry attached to it.

But if you *want* to present your daughter with a purity ring or necklace, I recommend a Christian jewelry organization in San Diego, California, by the name of Factory 79. You can reach them by telephone at 1-800-677-0832, or you can fax them at 1-888-349-7979. If you ask for a free brochure, they'll send you information on a full selection of available purity jewelry.

Some Inside Info

I like to wear a True Love Waits ring so the teens I speak with and minister to will know that I, too, am committed to sexual purity. I want them to know that I'm in the same ball game they're in.

I'm still single—never been married—and am still waiting on God to send Mr. Right into my life. But until He does, I am committed to remaining a virgin and maintaining my sexual purity until I'm married. I've had a lot of wonderful Christian dating relationships, but I've never gone past a kiss. And you know what? I'm so glad! I have absolutely no regrets! I can enter a lifetime of marriage without thinking, *If only I'd never . . .*

God can provide this same strength for your daughter. Teach her that her security, confidence, joy, and fulfillment will not come

> "I don't always want answers to my problems—just someone to talk to. But don't pressure me into talking about something when I'm in a bad mood and don't want to talk. Be patient with me. I'll talk when I'm ready."
>
> Abbie, seventeen

from a man. Teach her, Mom, that all this will only come from a strong, solid, intimate, growing relationship with Jesus Christ. Yes, a man can *enhance* her wholeness; but no human being can make another one whole. That's where dependence on God comes in.

Maintaining the Commitment

Once your daughter makes a pledge to save herself until marriage, how can you help her keep that oath? In other words, how can you help her be successful in living out her promise?

Let's take the word *pledge* and use it as an acrostic to create your strategy, okay?

P: Pledge. Emphasize the holiness of this pledge with your daughter. Again, it's not simply one more promise among many that she's made. It truly is a sacred oath to the King of kings!

Look up the word *oath* together and discuss its seriousness. Next, look up scriptures that talk about an oath and discuss these verses. Here are a few to get you started: Deuteronomy 6:18, 7:8; Psalm 119:106; Psalm 132:11; and Matthew 5:33.

Next, look up the word *covenant* and discuss its meaning. Read the following scriptures together: Genesis 9:9; Hebrews 8:8; 1 Corinthians 11:25; and Matthew 26:28.

L: Live it out! Talk with your daughter about the importance of not only *making* a pledge but living it out in every area of her life. What will this include? Make a list. Get specific. How will this affect her dating life? The movies she watches? The movies you watch?

E: Expect to be ridiculed and misunderstood. Living a sexually pure life in an immoral world is radical! By being a virgin and by choosing to remain pure in every area of her life, she'll naturally attract some attention. How can you prepare her for the hard times, the pressure, and the temptation to compromise? Ask her to allow you to support her daily in prayer and accountability. Ask her to come to *you* when she's tempted to give in and when she wonders if it's really worth it. Let her know she's not alone!

D: *Date only Christians.* God doesn't call us to "missionary dating." In other words, He doesn't expect your daughter to date a nonbeliever in order to bring that guy into a relationship with Him. God has a million and one ways to reach that boy. He can easily send another guy along his path . . . or even cause the rocks to cry out if He so desires. Leading non-Christian guys to the Lord is not your daughter's responsibility. So why date them?

Yes, Christ wants us to be friendly, loving, and kind to *everyone,* but there's a difference between being kind and establishing an intimate friendship.

Teach your daughter how to be selective. Let her know it's attractive to be choosy. She deserves the best! By waiting to date only guys who share her faith and morality, she's setting her standards high—and that's exactly where God wants them!

G: *Give God complete control of your love life.* Remind your daughter that her heavenly Father wants her fulfillment even more than she does! There's no relationship she could put together or work out better than He could. He's the Master. And He wants total control of your daughter's life—including her love life.

E: *Explain your boundaries.* It's important that your daughter not only *know* what her boundaries are but be able to *explain* them as well. The time to decide how far she'll go physically is not when she's alone on a date; it's *right now!*

But What If . . .

Perhaps you're thinking, *All that* sounds *good, but my daughter has already blown it.*

Are the two of you praying together? I truly believe in God's forgiveness and grace. I believe He can bestow "secondary virginity" on a young lady who has gone too far. We serve a God who will not only forgive but will also *forget!* Has your daughter sought His forgiveness?

Can I challenge you to pray *with* her? Explain to her that true repentance means "I don't ever plan on going down that road again." Not "I'll get forgiven now . . . and when I mess up again I'll come back and get some more." Yes, God will forgive and forgive. But that kind of thinking isn't coming from a repentant heart. That's coming from a mind of someone who wants to be temporarily free of guilt so she can go have her own way and continue in a vicious cycle of selfishness and sin.

> *"I love it when my mom dresses young and fashionably."*
>
> Becca, seventeen

Have you helped your daughter set boundaries for her dating life? I received a letter from a younger teen girl awhile back that stated, "My parents were gone, and my boyfriend came over to the house to study. After a while, he said he was hungry, so I told him to go into the kitchen and get something. He came back with a frozen hot dog and forced it up me! I was screaming and telling him to stop, but he wouldn't. I don't get it. What did I do wrong?"

My heart broke for this thirteen-year-old girl who obviously was a victim and who was absorbed in false guilt. She didn't give me her address, so I had no way of responding to her, but I would have loved to have told her she was not at fault.

At the same time, though, I can't help but think about her parents. Had they not given her any boundaries? Were there any rules concerning boys in the house? Of course, we all know that teens can still break rules behind parents' backs, but if they know there are rules with consequences, oftentimes they're more hesitant to go against their parents' expectations.

When I was a teenager, I knew beyond all doubt I could *never* go to a boy's house if his parents weren't home. I also wasn't allowed to have a guy over to my house without Mom or Dad being present. I remember thinking, *Oh brother! That's ridiculous. I only date Christian guys from the youth group. Nothing's gonna happen!*

And though nothing probably *would* have happened, I now see the wisdom in that rule. Why place myself—or a guy—in a situation where one of us *could* be tempted? It's simply not worth the risk.

What guidelines, boundaries, and rules have you given your daughter? What's permissible and what's non-negotiable? If you've never given her boundaries, don't be surprised if she's confused on the sexual purity issue and assuming it's all just about not having intercourse.

What about Victims?

Unfortunately, many of our daughters fall victim to sexual crimes every day. I cohost a national weekly radio show for teens. *Life on the Edge: LIVE!* is sponsored by Focus on the Family and is a call-in show.

Every Saturday night, our phone lines are barraged with calls from teens asking everything from A to Z. Sometimes we rejoice with them as they share the exciting things God is doing in their lives. Other times, we weep with them as they share deep hurts.

I'll never forget Haley's call. "I made a commitment to sexual purity when I was twelve," she said. "And when I was thirteen, my mom gave me a purity ring. I'm sixteen now, but three weeks ago I was raped by four guys in my neighborhood."

She began to cry as she continued the story. "I'm getting some counseling, and I think it will eventually help, but why I'm calling is . . . well, I'm wondering if . . . um, I haven't worn my purity ring since it happened. And, uh, I'm wondering . . . do you think God would mind if I started wearing it again?"

As best as I could, I hugged Haley over the phone lines and across the miles. "Of course you can, Haley. You were a victim. An awful crime was committed against you. You made a pledge to remain sexually pure until marriage, and in God's eyes you're still sexually pure. When He looks at you, He sees a princess wearing white. You are clean. You are pure. You are so loved by Him."

We prayed together, and eventually we had to hang up. But I've thought about Haley often, and I pray for her continued healing.

Another call comes to mind: "Susie, this is Reanna. Um . . . my pastor has been molesting me for the last couple of years. He kept saying it was okay, but I recently gave my life to Christ, and I know it's *not* okay. Will you pray with me?"

We prayed. Then I told her to close her eyes and pretend she was in my rocking chair. "If you were here," I said, "I'd wrap my afghan around you, and I'd sing." Then—even though it felt a little foolish to sing on the radio—I managed to get out the little chorus "God will make a way where there seems to be no way."

If your daughter has been victimized, she needs to be held by you. She also needs Christian counseling. How you help her handle the trauma will make or break the next several years for her. Pray with her. Ask Christ to begin the healing process she needs right *now*. Love her. Hug her. Hold her. Affirm her. Pour yourself into her soul . . . and walk through the healing process *together*.

☼ *Wrapping It Up* ☼

Mom, it's God's will that your daughter lives a sexually pure life. What, specifically, are you doing to enhance that? Are you monitoring TV, movies, magazines, friends, and dating relationships? Again, have you helped her establish physical and emotional boundaries?

Let me encourage you to pray with her about her future spouse. Make a list together of all the important qualities she needs in a husband. Give that list to God and trust Him with your daughter's love life.

I've written a few other things on this subject. If you're interested in more reading material, check out the following:

- *What Hollywood Won't Tell You about Sex, Love and Dating* by Greg Johnson and Susie Shellenberger (Regal Press, 1994)

- *Anybody Got a Clue About Guys?* by Susie Shellenberger (Servant, 1995)

- *Guys and a Whole Lot More* by Susie Shellenberger (Fleming-Revell, 1994)

- *258 Great Dates While You Wait* by Susie Shellenberger and Greg Johnson (Broadman and Holman, 1995)

- *Adventures in Singlehood* by Susie Shellenberger and Michael Ross (Zondervan, 1996)

Father, I want so badly to be the holy, godly, and pure example my daughter needs. Help me to be ever so cautious about all that I watch and listen to so I can be a mirror that reflects Your holiness.

Jesus, I also realize that the kind of friendships my daughter establishes with the opposite sex will have a giant effect on the kind of dating relationships she has. And the kind of dating relationships she has will, to some degree, determine the kind of marriage she ends up with. Help me to show her how to set her standards high, Father. Help me to verbalize what You and I expect from her.

And may she see You living and active in my lifestyle. Amen.

☀ *Memorize It . . . with Your Daughter* ☀

But among you there must not be even a hint of sexual immorality, or of any kind of impurity, or of greed, because these are improper for God's holy people. (Ephesians 5:3)

It is God's will that you should be sanctified; that you should avoid sexual immorality; that each of you should learn to control his own body in a way that is holy and honorable, not in passionate lust like the heathen, who do not know God; and that in this matter no one should wrong his brother or take advantage of him. (1 Thessalonians 4:3–6)

See that no one is sexually immoral. (Hebrews 12:16)

Friends Are Friends Forever?

*Helping Your Teen Daughter Understand
the Intricacies of Friendship Will Help
Her Establish Solid Relationships throughout Her Life*

You overhear your sixteen-year-old daughter, Terra, slam the phone in its cradle and murmur, "Crystal's no fun any more!"

"What are you talking about?" you inquire. "You love Crystal. You two are always up to something."

"I know. I don't get it. I asked her to come over and watch *The Princess Bride* with me, and she said she has other stuff to do."

"Didn't you two just watch that a couple of nights ago?"

"Yeah, but it's my favorite! She could watch it again with me!"

You think for a second then continue. "And what did you two do last weekend?"

"You remember, Mom. I needed a new pair of jeans, so she helped me find a pair at the mall."

"And you two were together yesterday afternoon too, weren't you?"

"Yeah, I needed help with my algebra, so I asked her to come over."

"Terra, it *could* be you're wearing Crystal out."

"What are you talking about, Mom?"

"Honey, it sounds like you're making several withdrawals from this friendship without putting in many deposits. You're *getting* a lot from Crystal, but you're not *investing* much in *her*."

The Friendship Account

Besides her family and her relationship with Christ, your daughter's friends will play the most important role in her life during her teen years. The key is to help her keep her friendships in balance so they won't become more important than family or God.

Right *now* is a great time to teach your teen daughter the important balance in good, solid friendships. Try to get her to see a healthy friendship as a stable bank account. We can't make continual withdrawals without putting in consistent deposits, or we'll go bankrupt.

Unfortunately, during the teen years, most adolescents are prone to self-centeredness—thinking mainly of themselves. Encourage your daughter to be the kind of friend whom everyone wants. What kind of friend is that? One who genuinely cares about those around her.

Being a Winning Friend

Teach your daughter (by example) that everyone loves to have a friend who's not simply interested in herself. Suggest these smart strategies for becoming a winning friend.

Invest interest. Encourage your daughter to show genuine interest in her friends. Memorize Philippians 2:4 together: "Don't just think about your own affairs, but be interested in others, too, and in what they are doing" (TLB).

Probably the easiest way to develop her interest in others is to teach her to ask meaningful questions. This will bring out what's important to her friends. A friendship without intention to grow and deepen becomes routine and eventually fades.

Listen to your friends. Teens are professionals at tuning stuff out. Teach your daughter to really *listen* to her friends. It's tempting for a teen to *look* at a friend but actually be thinking about last night's homework or what she wants to say as soon as she can jump into the conversation. And remind her that good listening requires eye contact with her friends. If you catch her playing with her hair or looking at her shoes, encourage her, instead, to look in the eyes of the friend who's speaking.

Make an investment of faith. Challenge your daughter to bring Jesus into each one of her friendships. Allow her to bring visitors to church and youth group—even when it means you have to drive an extra twenty minutes to pick someone up. Encourage her to pray for her friends and to share favorite Scriptures with them.

> "I wish my mom wouldn't ask 60 million questions when I'm telling a story."
> Heather, sixteen

So Little Time . . . So Many Friends

It's likely that the friends your daughter makes during her junior-high years won't be her friends for a lifetime. And though she *feels* like her high-school pals will be around forever, she'll actually only maintain a few of those friendships. *Most* of the friendships she'll take through life are the ones she'll make during her college time and the years after.

But it's important to begin teaching her how to develop great friendships *now*, so that when she *does* make the friends who will last for years, she'll understand the elements in nurturing them.

To do this, help your daughter understand the differences that exist in the types of relationships we form: *acquaintances* (people we know well enough to say hi to), *friends* (established from time spent together and talking), and *valued others* (require vulnerability, nurturing, and common depth).

> "My mom always gets frustrated with me when she knows something is bugging me and I don't tell her. She doesn't understand that many times I can't even verbalize it. It takes me at least a day or two sometimes before I can even label what I'm feeling."
>
> Erica, fourteen

Stress that it's good to have as many *acquaintances* as possible—to be friendly with everyone. And affirm your daughter in spending time with *friends* who are positive and share your value system. But teach her to choose her *valued others* wisely. These are the relationships you want to help her be selective about. Teach her that being choosy in this area is extremely wise. Because it's with these *valued others* that she'll share her heart, her values, and her secrets. And probably her life. Make it your prayer that her future spouse will be her soul mate—one who has grown from a *valued-other* friendship.

Communication

Oh, Diary!

It's like Mom is from another GALAXY. I mean, most of the time we don't even speak the same language. It's totally WEIRD. We'll be in the same room, and we're talking, but she doesn't even hear what I'm saying. And when she does hear it, she doesn't get it!

Most of the time, no one understands me except my FRIENDS.

Gotta go. I'm supposed to drive Jeremy to football practice.

Okay, Diary:

Here's the bottom line: I want to talk to Mom and Dad. I really do. But it's just so hard. Why don't they get it? Why don't they get anything?

Okay, so I'd never admit this to another human, but I guess it's safe in here . . . sometimes I'd give anything to be able to sit down and talk to them like, you know,

REAL PEOPLE.

And sometimes I wonder about stuff . . . like . . . what was Mom like when she was a teen? DID SHE BATTLE THE CRAMPS? Was she ever given detention? DID SHE HAVE LOTS OF FRIENDS? Whom did she have a crush on? What'd she do to get a guy's attention? WAS SHE EVER PRESSURED TO DRINK or smoke or have sex or say bad words or cheat or lie, or scared to stand in front of the class to give an oral report?

Sigh.

Guess I'll never know.

It's too much work . . . this communication thing.

Communication 101

Try to remember that as tough as it sometimes is for you to understand your teen daughter, it's equally as hard for her to understand you!

Moms, let's take a quick quiz to see how you're relating to your daughter, okay?

1. As soon as my daughter comes through the front door,
   a. I ask her to fold the laundry, do the dishes, or help with dinner.
   b. I ask her how her day was.
   c. I give her some time to unwind, then I ask her about homework.

2. When I want to know what happened during her day,
   a. I say, "Anything happen today that you want to talk about?"
   b. I say, "How was your day?"
   c. I say, "What's the best thing that happened today?" After she answers, I ask, "And what was the worst thing that happened today?"

3. The amount of time my daughter and I spend in actual conversation with each other every week:
   a. Fifteen minutes.
   b. Thirty-two minutes.
   c. At least an hour.

4. When my daughter says, "I don't know," it usually means:
   a. She really doesn't know.
   b. She knows but doesn't want to talk about it.
   c. She either really doesn't know or she's not ready to talk it out yet.

5. I know what my daughter's top three fears are.

    a. Not a clue.

    b. Probably.

    c. I'm pretty sure I know what they are.

SCORING:

If you scored mostly A's: Wake up, Mom! Introduce yourself to your daughter and start *really* trying to get to know one another. When she arrives home from school or work, don't pounce on her with questions about a lot of stuff, and don't immediately start giving her the chore list. Give her a chance to unwind first. Affirm her. Compliment her. Hug her. And about the last question . . . knowing what your daughter's afraid of will tell you a lot! You need to invest more time in her life.

If you scored mostly B's: You're trying, Mom, but you're not always thinking before you speak or act. Chances are, you're not the first one she turns to when her world caves in on her. Spend more time together. Ask questions that require more than a short answer. Ask her opinions. Discover who her favorite bands are. Do something fun together. You have a relationship, but it's not as close as it *could* be.

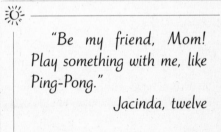

"Be my friend, Mom! Play something with me, like Ping-Pong."

Jacinda, twelve

If you scored mostly C's: You and your daughter have a pretty tight relationship, don't you? You know when to approach her, and you know when to back off. You're also good at "reading" your daughter, and that's so important in a close relationship. Continue to remind her how important she is to you, and your relationship will continue to grow.

Communication? What's That?

It happens all the time—you'll *say* one thing, but your daughter will *hear* something entirely different. Do any of these scenarios sound familiar?

You said: "Honey, why don't you try parting your hair?"
She heard: "Your hair looks awful! Can't you think of anything to do with it?"

You said: "Do you have homework tonight?"
She heard: "If I don't ask you about homework, you'll obviously forget all about it."

You said: "Who was on the phone?"
She heard: "Now who are you talking to? Anyone you're not supposed to?"

You said: "Why don't you invite a friend to come over and watch a movie Friday night after the game?"
She heard: "Since no one is going to ask you to do anything with them, you might as well spend the evening here at home with anyone you can talk into coming with you."

You said: "How was youth group?"
She heard: "I want to make sure you really went, so prove it by telling me what the youth pastor talked about tonight."

Teens don't always say exactly what they mean. Sometimes your daughter expects you to read between the lines. This takes practice and a lot of hard work. How well do you know what she's *really* saying? Do any of these statements and their *real* meaning sound familiar?

She said: "I had a rotten day!"
She meant: "My life is over!"

She said: "My hair won't do anything right!"
She meant: "Everyone is going to laugh at me for the rest of my life if you don't help me do something cool with my hair!"

She said: "I don't like that dress anymore."
She meant: "I feel so fat in that stupid dress! Everyone is looking at me and wondering how in the world I'll ever get it peeled off!"

She said: "There's a new boy at school."
She meant: "He's really cute, and how can I get his attention?"

She said: "Want me to make dinner tonight?"
She meant: "Can I borrow the car and ten dollars and spend the night at Tiffany's?"

She said: "Everyone else is!"
She meant: "Trust me, please. Give me a little more freedom. If I blow it, take it away."

She said: "Wanna go shopping?"
She meant: "Would you like to buy me a new pair of jeans and a sweater?"

She said: "When are we gonna do something?"
She meant: "Hey, we need to spend some time together. Can we talk?"

As a parent, there are certain things you probably dream of hearing your daughter tell you. And by working hard at communicating effectively, she *will* eventually say a lot. You both will. But here are some things *you'll probably never hear your daughter say* . . . so don't hold your breath!

- "I think my music is a little loud. I'm going to turn it down a few decibels. If it's still too loud, I'll use headphones from now on."

- "Mom, you've worked all day. I've only been to school. Let me wash the dishes tonight. Then I'll start on the laundry."

- "I noticed the grout in the shower is looking a little crusty, so I'm going to spend next Saturday cleaning it . . . if that's okay with you."

- "This movie I'm watching is pretty funny, but I'm thinking it would probably be more beneficial for all of us if we'd just turn off the TV and spend some time in prayer."

- "If any of my friends call, please tell them I can't talk tonight. I really need to concentrate on my homework."

- "I'd like to share more openly with you."

- "Do we really need this TV and VCR?"

- "I have some extra cash. Do you need anything?"

- "I was planning to go on a rafting trip next summer with some of the teens from church. But let's do something as a family instead. Is there a museum you'd like to visit?"

- "Hmmm. I'm thinking my dress is a little too short. I sure don't want guys getting the wrong message."

But . . . here are a few things your daughter would love to hear *you* say:

- "Honey, if we moved your bed a little closer to the wall, I think we could scoot a big-screen TV in here for you."

- "I just got a full tank of gas in case you'd like to use the car tonight."

- "Your dad and I will be gone Friday night. Wanna have a party while we're away?"

- "I'm thinking a fourth pierce in your left ear would look great on you!"

- "Why don't you get your tongue pierced at the same time?"

- "No, that's okay. I don't need to know where you're going all the time or whom you're with. I trust you."

- "Honey, you look really sleepy. Why don't you stay home from school today?"

- "All black could look really good on you."

- "None of your teachers are being unfair or expecting too much from you, are they?"

- "I forgot you don't like chicken-fried steak. Here, let me make you a hot-fudge sundae instead."

Getting Her to Talk

It's tough to develop good communication with your daughter if she's not wanting to talk. But helping her open up with you doesn't have to be as tough as it sounds. Let's think it through. You probably already have a few things to your advantage that you may not be seeing as opportunities.

Take carpooling, for example. I know, I know. It probably ranks pretty close to changing a flat tire, getting a run in your stockings, or cleaning the hamster's cage. But think again. Even though playing taxi driver to your daughter's soccer games, piano lessons, and play practices is time consuming and usually considered a hassle, where else can you have a closed-door, private conversation with your daughter as a captive audience?

Behind Locked Doors

Unlike when she's in the house, in the car your daughter can't escape to another room when you want to talk about something specific or confront her with specifics. Face it—you've got a captive audience!

"Mom, help me with my hair for a big school dance!"
Ivette, thirteen

There's also something a little less threatening about being inside a moving vehicle that allows more openness than sitting across from someone in a small room. Take advantage of this special time with your daughter to talk about private matters, bring up questions you think she might have about the opposite sex, or ask her what you can be praying with her about.

Learn from Her Friends

Driving your daughter and her pals is also a terrific time simply to *listen*. Where else can you be privy to her conversations with her closest friends? It's as though you're a little mouse hiding in the corner of the girls' locker room. What are they talking about? What is your daughter insecure and confident about? Do you notice that she tends to "go along" with the flow of conversation—even when it veers off-course from Christlike chatter? Or does she take the lead and present a contagious positive attitude? These are great observations to discuss with her later when it's just the two of you.

What are her friends saying? "I heard you can't take a bath when you're having your period," Sarah announces from the back seat.

"Did you know that if you sleep in a bra, your breasts won't grow?" Chelsey chimes in.

Make a mental note of anything incorrect you're hearing. If you've established a good rapport with her friends, this would be a great time to set the record straight by sharing your knowledge. You can be the wise hero in front of your daughter's friends.

Instead of going through the grocery list in your mind, tune in to what they're saying about Josh or Derek. You're not just a cab driver—you're in a top-notch position to glean valuable information that can draw you closer to your daughter.

Timing Is Everything

Of course, the car isn't the *only* place you can invest in some treasured talk with your daughter. There are obviously several other ways you can encourage her to share what's happening in her life with you, but atmosphere and timing *can* count for a lot! Here are some suggestions:

After lights out. Often times, teens are more comfortable talking about personal matters after they're in bed. It's dark, and you can't see whether their face is red or if they're nervous. There's a security that comes with being underneath a blanket and in your own bed. If you'll make the time to sit on the floor next to your daughter's bed, this can become a wonderful setting for heart-to-heart sharing.

When she's winning. Did your daughter make an A on that English test she was worried about? Did she win her basketball game? After she's had a successful experience, she'll feel more confident and willing to talk. Take advantage of these moments.

Around the supper table. Dinnertime can go either way. It's up to you—as a mom—to help set the right atmosphere for open sharing. Instead of asking general questions like "Do you have homework?" or "How was your day?" try to be specific. Parents are understandably frustrated when their teens respond with grunts and one-word answers. So give them an easy opening into an actual conversation. "What was the toughest part of your history exam?" challenges your daughter to think and search for an answer that can melt into a discussion.

When she's happy. When your daughter is having a good day, she's more likely to open up and share her heart with you. Look for these moments, but don't rely solely on them. In other words, though she may be more talkative when everything is going right, she may *need* to talk when things *aren't* going well. Your strategy? To provide a secure atmosphere where nothing is off-limits. Help your daughter know that the two of you can talk about *anything*—that there's nothing too weird, stupid, or "dirty" to discuss between the two of you.

Don't Expect Too Much

Though every mom wants a close relationship with her daughter, know there will be moments when the timing just isn't right for a heart-to-heart. For instance, when she's in a hurry isn't a good time to dissect her feelings. If she's rushed for time, she's already preoccupied with other things. Wait.

Don't try to persuade her to share her feelings with you when you're angry. You might regret your part of the conversation—and again, your goal is to provide a secure, loving atmosphere for openness.

There will be times when your daughter is full of explosive emotions— tears, giddiness, fear, anger. Allow her to vent—she needs that. But also realize that she may not be think- ing straight right now. Simply let her know she's

> "Please understand, Mom, that when I start spending more time with my friends, I still love you just as much; I'm only branching out."
> Cassandra, seventeen

loved and that you're there. When her emotions settle, you can talk about what was really bothering her and together come up with a way to confront the situation.

Good Communication

Honest sharing is born out of trust. Never make fun of your daughter or tease her about weight, boys, her complexion, or other personal things. This can destroy years of trust in a split second.

And if you're *not* communicating very well right now? Make it a matter of prayer, and start *doing* it. In other words, the more you communicate, the better a communicator you'll be!

Got Any Examples?

Let's hear from Meggan and P. J. Connelly, from Lancaster, Pennsylvania, a mom and daughter who *are* communicating effectively. Maybe you'll pick up a few hints that can enhance the communication lines between you and your daughter.

"When I was in the fourth grade, my father, Major Mark Connelly, M.D., was called up from the reserves to serve in the Gulf War. I had complete faith that my daddy would return home, but that faith was severely tested.

"On February 28, 1991, the day of cease-fire for Desert Storm, my dad was killed in action. Mom's optimistic attitude and faith in God's providence set an example and comforted me from the moment we were informed of his death. She held me in her loving arms as tears of sadness, loneliness, and frustration fell from my eyes.

"Many times she answered the question 'Why did Jesus have to take my daddy?' with the gentle reply 'Only God knows why, and He wants us to trust in His providential love.' Daily, she promises me that even though I can't see or hear my dad, he is closer to me now than he ever was before.

"I have a very fond memory of my mom's infectious optimism. I often wake up to my mom singing a song that she's written, 'It's going to be a good day today, a fine day today. . . .' And I'm reminded that with God's help I can face whatever the day brings. My mom has always encouraged me *not* to use my dad's death as an excuse—but to think big and strive to reach my dreams. Many evenings she stays up to help me with schoolwork or to listen to me play the piano. She often reminds me how proud my dad is of me.

"A treasure in my heart is the time I spend with my mom reading God's Word, praying, and learning how to become a godly woman. She has taught me that 'Charm is deceitful and beauty is passing, but a woman who fears the Lord, she shall be praised' (Proverbs 31:30). Mom has modeled 'the incorruptible beauty of a gentle and quiet spirit, which is very precious in the sight of God' (1 Peter 3:4).

"When I miss my dad, or I'm overwhelmed with fear and frustration, Mom encourages me to cling to God's promises, such as the one in Psalm 29:11: 'The Lord will give strength to His people, the Lord will bless His people with peace.'

"When my father was called up to serve in the Gulf War, my family memorized James 1:2–4: 'My brethren, count it all joy when you fall into various trials, knowing that the testing of your faith produces patience. But let patience have its perfect work, that you may be perfect and complete, lacking nothing.' God's Word has been our firm foundation every step of the way. Many nights as I crawl into bed I find a note from my mom, expressing the unconditional love that she and God have for me.

"It's hard to believe, but I can honestly say I am grateful for the lessons God has taught me through the death of my dad. I may never have known how special a mother's friendship could be. My mom and I share everything with each other—our frustrations, fears, joys, and tears. I believe she's a special gift from the Lord. Her positive encouragement, wise instruction, and godly example have brought me through the death of my father and into a closer relationship with God and my family."

Lessons to Learn

Did you catch some of the ingredients that comprise good, solid communication between Meggan and her mom?

- "She held me in her loving arms." Her mom was physically as well as emotionally involved in Meggan's life.

- "A treasure in my heart is the time I spend with my mom reading God's Word, praying, and learning how to become a godly woman." P. J. knows the value of making a spiritual investment in her daughter's life. She's also living a godly example in front of her daughter. Wouldn't it be great, like the apostle Paul, to be able to say to those around us, "Watch me and imitate me"? Wow. God wants your daughter to see *Him* through your life.

- "Many nights as I crawl into bed I find a note from my mom, expressing the unconditional love that she and God have for me." Meggan has a wise mom. Not only does she *tell* her daughter how special she is, but P. J. backs it up with special reminders that constantly point Meggan's focus back to the Lord.

- "Many evenings she stays up to help me with school-work or to listen to me play the piano." If it's important to Meggan, P. J. makes it important to *her*.

Is it any wonder that this mother/daughter relationship is tight? With such strong bonding, they'll be friends for life!

My Own Story

I never realized until I left home what an incredible privilege it was to have grown up in a godly family. My parents took my brother and me to church every time the doors were open. We also had family altar in the evenings. Praying together and opening God's Word as a foursome certainly helped plant a strong and positive interest toward spiritual matters.

Mother has always had an incredible knack for making the ordinary seem extremely special. Every single Saturday during my growing-up years, Mom would bake a chocolate cake for our family to eat during the week. She knew that no matter what I was doing (playing kickball, building forts, riding my bike), when the cake came out of the oven, I'd want a piece. She'd track me down—and sometimes I'd be half a block away in my own fantasy world. But I knew when she called, it meant my special opportunity for a piping-hot piece of homemade cake, fresh from the oven.

The same went for evening meals. Instead of always serving the same ol' boring thing the same ol'

> *"Mom, don't penalize me for being the oldest—I didn't ask to be born first."*
> *Rachel, sixteen*

way, she'd often pack everything up and set up housekeeping in the backyard so we could have an adventure meal. Dad would grill steaks or hot dogs outside, Mom would bake brownies and bring out the fly swatter, and we'd build a memory together.

"I'm Bored!"

I get bored easily—and my childhood was no exception. I always wanted to be doing something. I can remember sweltering-hot, humid Oklahoma summer days when Mom would haul our croquet set out of the attic, set it up in the backyard, and challenge me to "tournaments."

When we got bored with croquet, we'd pull out Trouble—you know, the board game with the pop-up plastic bubble in the middle? And we'd start another tourney. We'd even chalk our scores on a little blackboard on the wall. No matter what it was—checkers, Sorry, croquet, fun dinners—Mom made it special. She always went the extra mile.

Just Us

When I was a freshman in high school, I had piano lessons every Monday at 4:30. My brother had late basketball practice and other stuff, and my dad taught a Monday evening college class. So Mom invented a weekly tradition that involved just the two of us.

Each week, the newspaper ran a coupon for a "buy one—get one free" dinner at the Jolly Roger restaurant in Oklahoma City. After piano, Mother would pick me up and treat me to whatever I wanted at Jolly Roger. I can't remember what we talked about or what we ordered. I just know it meant the world to me that Mom and I had a special time together each week. She made me feel important. And that breeds security. And confidence. And a whole lot of other healthy characteristics. For that, I'll always be grateful.

☼ Wrapping It Up ☼

Are there some specific things you can do to develop a deeper relationship with your daughter? As your relationship grows, your communication naturally deepens. Make time to remind your daughter *often* how incredibly special she is. Spend time with her. Let there be no doubt in her mind of the important role she plays in your life.

Father, I confess there are times when I don't really listen to my daughter. Help me not only to see her needs but to focus on them and to grow closer to her because of them.

I really want an intimate relationship with my daughter, Lord. And it's so important to me, I'll do whatever You show me to do. I'm realizing more and more that I only have a few years with her, and I want them to really count. I want her to be able to look back and recall my encouragement, my hugs, my notes, and my prayers. Teach me how to be more disciplined at showing her how much I care.

Thank You, Father.

Amen.

☼ Memorize It . . . with Your Daughter ☼

I thank my God every time I remember you. In all my prayers for all of you, I always pray with joy because of your partnership in the gospel from the first day until now, being confident of this, that he who began a good work in you will carry it on to completion until the day of Christ Jesus. It is right for me to feel this way about all of you, since I have you in my heart. (Philippians 1:3–7)

We always thank God for all of you, mentioning you in our prayers. We continually remember before our God and Father your work produced by faith, your labor prompted by love, and your endurance inspired by hope in our Lord Jesus Christ. (1 Thessalonians 1:2–3)

And this is my prayer: that your love may abound more and more in knowledge and depth of insight, so that you may be able to discern what is best and may be pure and blameless until the day of Christ, filled with the fruit of righteousness that comes through Jesus Christ—to the glory and praise of God. (Philippians 1:9–11)

The Opposite Sex . . . and Your DAUGHTER!

Though This Is Often a Roller-Coaster Season for Teen Girls, It Doesn't Have to Be!

Twelve-year-olds Allison and Sabrina go to the same church and the same school and are in the same class. Allison thinks boys are gross. "They make weird noises, they're loud, and they always need a bath," she says.

Sabrina, however, can't wait to get home from school, pick up the phone, and start calling every boy in her zip code. "Jeremy's to die for!" she exclaims. "And Bryan is soooo good at soccer. My heart skips a beat every time I watch him play."

What's wrong with this picture? How can two girls—the same age—be on totally different timetables?

As parents, you're already keenly aware that children mature at different rates physically. Teens mature at different rates emotionally. Because our heavenly Father has wired each of His children individually and uniquely, there *is* no perfect time for a teen to start blossoming emotionally. But it *will* happen. And when Allison finally *does* notice guys, how are you going to handle it?

Focus on the Big Picture

You can help your teen daughter keep the whole "guy thing" in perspective by teaching her the difference between fleeting emotions and solid commitment. Her heart may flutter when Judson walks by, but that's not love. Love is commitment centered on an intimate relationship with Christ.

There's a movement today among Christians called courtship. Perhaps you've heard of it. Even in the Christian community, there are differing views about it. Allow me to explain briefly.

Courtship advocates believe that teens shouldn't date simply to date. "Why allow yourself to be in a series of relationships that break your heart, harden your emotions, and only prepare you for short-term relationships?"

The other camp would say that's merely a part of growing up—that we can't prevent our children from being hurt.

Those behind the courtship movement ask, "Why date if you're not ready to get married?" They suggest not involving yourself in a guy/girl relationship until you're emotionally and spiritually ready to make a lifetime commitment.

Your Family

I don't know what views *you* hold, but allow me to make a couple of suggestions, okay?

Form fantastic friendships. Whether you're a courtship advocate or a supporter of traditional dating relationships, teach your daughter how to establish quality friendships with the opposite sex. And help her realize the difference between friendships and relationships. It's possible to be friendly without flirting. There's a difference between knowing good social skills—being able to carry on a quality conversation with the opposite sex —and chasing the opposite sex. Help your daughter realize that friends of both sexes are valuable and to be treasured.

Guard your heart. Though it would be impossible to keep your daughter's heart from being bruised (even from everyday occur-rences), you *can* teach her that what goes on in her heart and in her mind are connected. That's why the Bible tells us to guard our heart—for it is the well-spring of life. In other words, what happens in the heart will often transfer to the mind and eventually manifest itself through actions.

> "Mom, I need to feel my way. Don't give me a solu-tion to everything. Give me the tools to make my own decisions. If I get hurt, nei-ther of us is going to die— I'll learn from it."
>
> *Perri, eighteen*

To live a holy life, our hearts must be guarded. The best way this can happen is if we allow the Holy Spirit to control our heartstrings. Pray with your daughter. Work hard to maintain an open relationship with her. Encourage her to tell you what she's thinking and feeling.

Boys Are Not the Enemy

Your goal as a parent is to help your daughter establish *healthy* friendships with the opposite sex. Teach her that the kind of friendships she builds with guys will probably be the kind of mar-riage she ends up with some day. Therefore, whether she's dating, courting, or simply being a good friend, encourage her to make

Jesus Lord of all her relationships. This will change the focus from "Does he like me?" and "How can I get him to notice me?" to "How can I encourage him in his walk with God?"

Bottom line: The opposite sex isn't the bad guy. It's how we treat each other and what develops between us that is either good or becomes questionable. Be there for your daughter. Keep her talking with you. And *always* saturate her with prayer.

Giving Your Daughter a Spiritual Heritage

Good ol' Diary:

I just assumed that all my FRIENDS at church prayed with their parents. But Jessalyn was talking today about how her parents said they prayed for her but she never hears them pray for her or sees them doing it.

Wow.

GUESS I HAVE A LOT TO BE THANKFUL FOR.

Sometimes I get frustrated when Dad interrupts my homework and calls us all into the dining room to pray, but I'm really glad he does. It feels so secure to kneel together as a family. Even though we don't do it every night, I know my parents believe in the power of prayer.

MAYBE THAT'S WHY IT'S EASY FOR ME TO PRAY.

Hmmm.

Diary Dearest:

This morning I told Jessalyn that she oughtta just ask her parents if they can all pray together. She said it sounded like a good idea but she'd feel totally weird trying to pull it off.

I can't even imagine that. It feels so natural for Mom and Dad and Jeremy and me to pray together. Even when we're not praying together, I've seen Mom sitting in her rocker late at night reading the Bible and bowing her head. I know she's praying for me. And I know she's praying for the little stuff too.

You know, my speech for junior-class treasurer, that I'll find the right homecoming dress. But she also prays about the big things— Mr. Hildebrand giving me a hard time, and Mrs. Owens, and that part-time job I needed.

Sometimes after I'm already in bed, she'll stop by my room, and she thinks I'm asleep. I lie totally still and pretend I'm way gone, but I feel her kneeling next to my bed, and I hear her whisper my name to God.   Wow.   I totally luuuuv that.

It makes me feel that no matter how many times my world caves in on me . . . everything's gonna be all right . . . . cuz Mom is praying.

LATER AND AMEN.

Making a Spiritual Investment

Leaving your daughter with a spiritual heritage is done through prayer, your relationship with Christ, and saturating yourself with the Bible. There's nothing more powerful than a mother's prayers. Does your daughter know you're praying for her? Are you also praying *with* her? I've mentioned that several times in this book, because I can't stress enough how incredibly important it is. Through your prayers, you're passing on a spiritual legacy to your daughter.

So . . . PRAY!

What should you pray about? Anything and everything! The big stuff and the little things. Attitudes, friendships, responsibility, grades, her future . . . you name it! Though there are millions of prayers that are important for your daughter, let me start you off with five prayers you absolutely-beyond-all-doubt gotta pray!

Pray for her salvation. When it's all said and done, the only thing that will matter is where your daughter will spend eternity. This should be the upmost important thing on

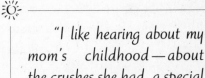

> "I like hearing about my mom's childhood—about the crushes she had, a special dance she went to, and how she and Dad got together."
>
> Tori, sixteen

your agenda, Mom! Make *sure* that you know that you know that you know your daughter has a vibrant, active, intimate, growing relationship with Jesus Christ. And if she doesn't? Keep praying!

My grandmother Dickerson died when she was ninety-six years old, and she prayed for me every single day of my life. My grandma

Shellenberger died when she was one hundred years old, and she prayed for me every single day of my life.

My parents also pray for me every single day of my life. I have aunts and other extended relatives who saturate my life with prayer. Do you know what that does for me? I mean . . . really? To *know* that people are going to the throne for me *daily!* What a spiritual heritage!

Not only do they pray for me, but they've told me all my life that they're praying daily for me. I've seen them pray, I've heard them pray, and they've prayed *with* me. What did that do for me when I was in high school? It kept me on the right track! I really never desired to rebel, but even if I had wanted to, I would have thought twice because so many people were paying such a high cost spiritually for me.

Can you imagine the difference it would make in your daughter's life to receive that kind of spiritual legacy from you? And the exciting part is . . . you can start right now! Maybe you're not as fortunate to have such a strong spiritual background, but *you* can *become* her spiritual background right now!

Pray for her to establish a strong, deep relationship with Jesus Christ. The desire of every mother's heart is to see her daughter grow deep roots in the Lord Jesus. There's something special about a spiritually strong teen girl—she matures into a spiritually strong young woman. And that young woman keeps maturing spiritually into a prayer warrior of a mom. And that mom becomes an intercessor for her grandchildren! It starts right now with you . . . and with your daughter.

Pray for her friends. My friend Lynda tells about her daughter Courtney's friend Shayla. "Susie, she really wasn't the type of girl I wanted Courtney hanging out with. Shayla's older sister had some previous problems with drugs, and I was just uncomfortable with the whole friendship," Lynda says.

"But as I began praying for Shayla, the Lord began speaking to me. Very clearly He said, 'Lynda, I love Shayla just as much as I love Courtney. Shayla needs Me.'"

I work with Lynda, but we attend different churches. One particular night, though, my church was having a special evangelistic drama that I thought she and her children would enjoy. I invited them, and since Shayla was staying at their house a few days while her mom was out of town, she naturally came with Courtney.

At the end of the presentation, an invitation was given for people to come forward and give their lives to Christ. Courtney says, "I'll never forget looking at Shayla and hearing her say, 'Courtney, will you walk up there with me? I want that.'"

Shayla accepted Christ that night.

"The next day I went to a Christian bookstore and bought her a leather-bound Bible and had her name engraved on the outside," Lynda says. "And that night as I gathered Shayla and my kids in my bedroom, I planned on showing her how to underline scriptures that had special meaning for her. But as I began our devotional time together, Courtney and her brother, Clint, just jumped in and took over. They gave her a highlighter and opened their own Bibles to show her what verses were special to them."

Shayla was not only getting to know Jesus Christ in a personal way, she was now on the right track to becoming discipled and

> "Sometimes I wonder . . . what was my mom like as a teen? Would she and I have been friends? I wish she'd talk to me about stuff like that."
>
> Allison, sixteen

learning how to grow in her faith. None of that would have happened if Lynda hadn't started praying for her daughter's friends.

Pray for your daughter's husband. I realize it may feel funny praying for someone you don't even know, but it matters. Ask God to help that young man grow strong in Him. Pray that *right now* he'll start becoming the godly man your daughter will need someday. And ask the Lord to begin the process *right now* of molding your daughter into the kind of wife that young man is going to need. Imagine how good it will feel to know, when your daughter gets married someday, that you've already made a strong spiritual investment in his life!

Pray for your daughter's protection—spiritual, emotional, and physical. I talked with Cassie Bernall's mom, Misty, recently. She said, "For some reason, I felt I needed to hug Cassie the morning she left for school and tell her I loved her." Misty, of course, had no idea that two high-school gunmen would make history that day inside the corridors of Littleton High School and that her daughter would be martyred for her faith.

We don't have any control over when or how God will allow our daughters to leave us and spend eternity with Him, but we do need to be interceding for them in consistent, daily prayer—several times throughout the day!

God's Word

You can also leave your daughter a spiritual heritage by having devotions with her and teaching her how to study and understand the Bible. Remember my friend Lynda whom I mentioned earlier? Having Bible study and prayer time is a daily occurrence in her home. It's a non-negotiable. It comes as naturally as breathing. How? Because she has instilled in her children the necessity of it!

"One day Ashley's friends were being really fickle," Lynda remembers. "So that night, as I gathered the kids into my room, we began looking up scriptures on friendship and talking about the difference between genuine friends and surface-level friends. I made some snacks, and we used a little dry-erase board to list the true characteristics of deep, long-lasting friends. It made all the difference for Ashley. We prayed for her friends, but she realized that even if her friends are here today and gone tomorrow, she'll always have her family."

Lynda always makes sure their devotional time is early in the evening and there are no distractions. "We turn off the television and the music," she says. "And if the phone rings, we let the machine pick it up. Nothing interrupts our time together with God."

She also chooses a comfortable spot in the house where the kids won't be restless. "Sometimes we meet in my bedroom, and we all crowd together on top of the bed. Other times, I'll make hot-chocolate and we'll gather around the table in the dining room or in front of the fireplace."

She keeps it short—fifteen to twenty minutes—and now that her kids are in their teen years, they're beginning to take ownership of this special time. "The other night I told Clint to get something ready for Bible study, and he decided to do something on prayer. He got the concordance out and had several verses for us to read. We discussed the power of prayer, marveled at how God used prayer through the Bible, and shared our own answers to prayer. Then we concluded by praying for each other."

Lynda's teens expect to have devotions as a part of their daily routine, because she's taken the time and energy to make it that.

Kathy has devotions with her daughter, Kelly, but they read a devotional book together. "She reads part of it aloud, and I read part of it aloud," Kathy says. "Then we both look up the scriptures that go along with the devotional thought, and we pray together.

The whole thing might last fifteen minutes. I don't want it to be too long that she gets bored. But it's just enough to connect *us* together and to connect us to Christ as a mom and daughter."

Think Kelly, Clint, Ashley, or Courtney will ever forget these devotional times? No way! While they may not remember each specific devotional study, they *will* remember the spiritual legacy their moms are building in their lives. Teaching your daughter to hide God's Word in her heart will last a lifetime!

Saturate with Scripture

Let's break it down even a little more. Let's say it's 10:30 A.M., and your fourteen-year-old daughter is almost in tears. She's heading from science class to history, and a couple of girls behind her have been making fun of her jeans. They're too short.

You'd give anything to be with her right now. To scoop her into your arms, pray together, and remind her that this truly isn't as big a deal as it seems.

But obviously, you can't do that. She's at school, and you're not. In fact, you're completely unaware that she's even *having* a crisis. So what's the answer?

The Word to the Rescue

If you can help your daughter hide God's Word in her heart, she won't panic when a crisis arises and you can't be there to help her through it. If you can teach her to file His resources in her mind, she'll always have something to reach for—to lean on—to bring her through even the most trying of times.

How can you accomplish this? The psalmist challenges us to hide God's Word in our hearts. He's not simply talking to teen girls; he's speaking to *all* Christians *everywhere*. So, it makes sense to practice this strategy in front of your daughter. She needs to see how important God's Word is in *your* life. Is she able to watch you apply Scripture to your lifestyle?

Self-Check Quiz

Let's take a quick little test to help assess some key issues before we go any further, okay?

Does your daughter see you reading the Bible during the week? Though you may have an incredible quiet time with the Lord behind closed doors, it's important that you take it into the living room or the kitchen once in a while. She needs to *see* you reading your Bible.

Does your daughter see you taking your Bible to church? It takes a special effort these days to do this, doesn't it? Most churches have Bibles available in the pew rack right next to the hymnal. So why lug *yours* to church if you can use one that's already there? Because the more your daughter sees you carrying your Bible around, the more she'll realize how important it is to you.

> "I wish my mom knew how very much I appreciate her."
>
> Michelle, thirteen

Does she see you looking to the Bible as merely a good book—as you would a novel—or does she sense from you that it's a sacred instruction manual that holds the solutions to every trial we'll ever face? When she sees you turn to God's Word during a crisis, she'll catch on that it holds the answers and guidance we need.

Does she know that reading and knowing the Bible are non-negotiable for growing Christians? Or does she have the idea that hearing it on Sundays will suffice? Hopefully, she's learning through you that Scripture provides the nutrition we need to develop strong spiritual muscles.

Wearing the Word

The Book of Ezekiel shows the prophet *eating* Scripture. Now granted, Ezekiel was famous for creative object lessons—seems he'd do almost anything to get people's attention so he could tell them about God. But I like to think Ezekiel *ate* the Word of God to show us that it's not enough simply to *read* the Bible. God wants us to *digest* it until it becomes a part of our lifestyle.

Teach your daughter that the Bible isn't just your Sunday reading—it's your ammunition, your vitamins, your fuel for living. When you get the raise you were praying for, let her see you open the Word and read scriptures of praise and thanksgiving.

When your heart is breaking over the death of a terminally ill friend, let her see you turn to the Bible for comfort.

When you're confused about a family decision—whether to sell the house or take the vacation or purchase that new car—let her watch you open the Word for guidance.

Bottom line: Saturate your life with Scripture. Quote it, sing it, memorize it, digest it, share it. Create some fun family challenges in putting the Bible to memory. And share those verses with each other on the drive to school, on your way to buy those new gym shoes, while you're waiting in line at the drive-through.

The more important God's Word becomes to your daughter, the less you'll have to worry about not being there for her. Why? Because she'll be able to reach inside her heart and pull out the exact word God has for her in every trial she faces.

☼ *Wrapping It Up* ☼

The most important thing you'll ever do for your daughter is measured in terms of what she'll remember after you're gone. And that's why passing on a spiritual heritage for her is so vitally important. No matter how much time or energy it takes—no matter what you need to sacrifice to do it—make sure it's done!

> *Oh, Father,*
>
> *I'm beginning to realize how vitally important it is that I leave my daughter with something that is immovable, unshakable, and everlasting. I want to leave her with a strong and rich spiritual heritage.*
>
> *Forgive me for not taking this responsibility more seriously. I'm beginning to realize that there are some things only I as her mother can give her. Lord, help me to be an open spiritual testimony for her. Give me the discipline and the desire to make the time to develop a consistent devotional life with her.*
>
> *I realize that, to a large degree, her spiritual depth will depend on me—how I challenge her, how I show her Your answers to prayer, how I explain the Scriptures to her.*
>
> *Father, I need Your strength and Your wisdom.*
>
> *I pledge to You that I will begin right now to pass on a spiritual heritage to my daughter.*
>
> *I love You, Jesus!*
>
> *Amen.*

☼ *Memorize It . . . with Your Daughter* ☼

Finally, be strong in the Lord and in his mighty power. Put on the full armor of God so that you can take your stand against the devil's schemes. For our struggle is not against flesh and blood, but against the rulers, against the authorities, against the powers of this dark world and against the spiritual forces of evil in the heavenly realms. (Ephesians 6:10–12)

Be very careful, then, how you live—not as unwise but as wise, making the most of every opportunity, because the days are evil. (Ephesians 5:15–16)

Therefore, my dear brothers, stand firm. Let nothing move you. Always give yourselves fully to the work of the Lord, because you know that your labor in the Lord is not in vain. (1 Corinthians 15:58)

Building Your Daughter's Confidence
In a World of Insecurity, You Can Make the Difference!

As a little girl, I believed I could do anything. Well . . . anything except stuff involving numbers. To this day, I'm still not any good at math, and I can't figure out a story problem to save my life.

But when it came time to take the training wheels off my bike, perform at piano recitals, create an oral report for school, learn to drive a stick shift, build relationships, stick with tough courses, complete a master's thesis, buy a home, or write a book, Mom and Dad always said, "You can do it. You can do anything you put your mind to, if you're willing to work hard enough."

For some reason, I believed them. Now, I don't know if it was done on purpose, but I like to think Mom and Dad had a great strategy. I like to think it was because of their consistent affirmation and their guidance in helping me establish a strong relationship with Christ that my teen years were never a nightmare. I also like to think that's one of the reasons I'm happy and content today.

Your Turn

I'm guessing the desire for your teen daughter to have a strong relationship with God and to become a confident young lady ranks extremely high on your priority list. But in a teen's world of insecurity and frightening statistics (every half-hour thirty-two teen girls in America have abortions and fifty run away from home), how can you accomplish this? Here are my suggestions.

Confidence is taught. Aggressively seek and find the things your daughter does well, and praise her. Does she empty the dishwasher without being asked? Maybe she takes great care of the family dog.

> *"Mom, if you'll tell me about embarrassing stuff that happened to you, I'll feel more comfortable talking about stuff that happens to me."*
>
> Anne, fourteen

Or perhaps she helps you with your younger children. Affirm her!

It's even possible that you're interpreting some of the things she's doing as negative or as a waste of time. Try to see the positive side of her interests. For example, her tying up the phone an hour every night can be frustrating! But bring out the positive side—let her know you think it's great that she cares so much about her friends.

As you teach your daughter to believe in herself, keep pointing her toward her Creator. The closer she grows to Jesus, the more clearly she knows who she is and Whose she is.

Convictions are learned. What is your daughter learning in your home about Christ? About the Bible? Are you aware of what she's being taught in Sunday school? Youth group? Bible study? If you simply assume she's learning Scripture-based convictions, don't. Find out firsthand.

I hope your daughter is learning not only *what* she believes but *why* she believes it. Can she articulate her faith? Does she know what the Word of God has to say about homosexuality, abortion, anger, and hell? Are you helping her learn about moral absolutes? Does she realize there *is* an absolute Truth? What she ultimately believes about God and the Bible will eventually be reflected in her character.

Character is built. If you try to build character without convictions, you end up with a phony. Every adult knows a teen who puts on an *act* of character around her parents yet when she's away from Mom and Dad folds up instead of holds up.

The best way to build character is by *living out* character in front of her. The apostle Paul challenged his young disciple Timothy to imitate him. Wow! That says a lot. Are you exhibiting such character that you can ask your daughter to imitate *you*? Does she know what convictions shape you and your husband's character? Discuss your convictions with her. Help her to see how your convictions and your character play off each other.

Your Daughter's Future

Much of your daughter's contentment, fulfillment, and confidence ten years from now is really being shaped *this very moment*. A confident *girl* with character built on biblical convictions will usually develop into a confident *woman*. Make it a goal to memorize Joshua 1:5–9 together, and live it!

Guiding Your Post-Teen Daughter

Di:

Can't believe I'm twenty years old and still telling you everything. I flipped back through your pages last week and got a few laughs from some of my early entries. What a kick!

Like I was really worried about my period? And tampons?

And Aaron—who in the world was that? Sheesh! I had his name scribbled all over the pages.

What a case I was!

Sigh.

And in some ways . . . I guess I still am a case.

Like with my life, I mean.

Here I am in college. My dream college. The place I've wanted to be since seventh grade. But now that I'm here, I'm thinking, *What am I doing here?*

I mean, shouldn't it be totally unfair to waste Mom and Dad's money on classes that I'm not sure are really gonna get me anywhere?

I just don't know what I want to do!

I feel so clueless.

Gotta meet Jenna at the Java Joint. See ya.

Grab the Goals

Teaching your daughter to set and reach goals can be fun! And if she's made it through her teen years and is still unsure about her life's direction, it's time to get serious about goal setting.

Stacie was probably the most talented teen in my youth group. She could act, sing, and write, genuinely cared about others, prayed with her peers, was an excellent role model, and was consistent in her walk with Christ.

It was easy to dream big dreams for her—it seemed she could do anything she wanted with her life. But as her senior year came to a close and I questioned her about the future, she seemed dazed.

I watched Stacie enter and graduate from college with no real goals. Afterward, she jumped from one job to another. She had no focus. I couldn't understand how someone so full of talent and skill could be so plagued with such lack of direction.

The more I watched Stacie and interacted with her, I began to realize that even though she could have done anything with her life, her parents had never taught her how to establish goals. No wonder she had zero ambition—she'd never been mentored in this area.

I'm convinced that other than helping our daughter establish an intimate, growing relationship with Christ, the second-most important thing we can do is teach her how to set and reach specific goals.

So Many Goals . . . So Little Time

What kind of goals? Where does one begin? What's really important? What should we be encouraging her to strive toward? Well, a lot of that is really up to you, Mom and Dad.

As parents, you have approximately eighteen years to help your daughter learn what's important. In other words, by the time she leaves your home and heads off to college, what do you want her to take with her?

As mentioned several times throughout this book, as Christian parents, I hope your first and foremost goal is that she will leave with a solid, personal relationship with Christ.

How does that happen? Again, spending daily time with our heavenly Father—through prayer and Bible reading—is an essential ingredient in a growing relationship with the Lord. This is a fantastic goal to begin with!

Help your daughter set a personal goal of reading her Bible and praying every single day. Even though she may be twenty years old right now, if she's still not in the habit of doing it, help her! How? Instead of setting a big goal of spending thirty minutes a day reading the Bible, encourage her to set a more attainable goal—one you know she can reach. Why not begin with a goal of one minute a day? *Anyone* can read the Bible for one minute a day! And anyone can pray for one minute a day.

> *"Know what I love about my mom? She'll always keep my secrets. I can tell her anything and she won't share with anyone. And she doesn't make fun of my crushes. I love it when she's supportive of me and when she tells me I made a good decision."*
>
> Roxanne, sixteen

After she successfully reaches that goal, it'll probably be a month or less before she's spending fifteen to twenty minutes a day in her devotional time—without even realizing it!

What Else?

What other goals do you want to help your daughter set and meet before leaving home? Again, as a parent, *you* have to answer that question. What has God laid on your heart that's important?

Here are a few ideas to start the wheels turning.

Money Goals: Tithing and Saving

My parents wanted to teach me the importance of using money wisely. They did this by beginning with tithing and saving. As a youngster, they taught me that God owns everything we have—but He only asks that 10 percent of what we earn be given back to Him in tithe. They helped me learn that this is essential for a growing church.

> *"My mom helps me think through stuff. She's really smart, and she's great at helping me see both sides and then giving me the freedom to choose."*
>
> Roxanne, sixteen

I'm glad I learned that principle early in life. As an adult, I never think twice about tithing. It's an automatic response. It's non-negotiable. It's the very first thing that comes off each paycheck I receive.

Sadly, I know adults who still struggle with this biblical principle. "If we have enough money after paying bills, we might be able to tithe this month," they reason. Unbeknownst to them, they're missing out on some exciting blessings and spiritual-growth lessons.

Immediately after tithe was taken care of, my parents taught me to save. Dad always said, "If you'll tithe ten percent and save ten percent, you'll more than likely do okay financially."

He was right. As an adult, I'm glad I know how to use money wisely. But I wouldn't know this if Mom and Dad hadn't helped me establish some financial goals.

Saving for Something Specific

Maybe your daughter wants a new car. How will she get it? Does she have a job? If not, encourage her to peruse the want ads. Does she have a resume? If not, challenge her to get a book on how to put a resume together.

If she already has a job, perhaps you need to show her how to budget wisely. Maybe she's spending too much on clothes right now to be able to set anything aside for a car. Go over her budget with her and make suggestions.

Responsibility

This goal can cover a wide array of things—responsibility with household chores (and yes, if she's still living in your house, she needs to help with chores), helping with food costs and utilities, etc.

Investing Her Life

Would you consider encouraging your daughter to set a goal for involvement in missions? Help her see the necessity of planning financially and preparing spiritually *now* for a summer that could impact the rest of her life. Who knows? One or two mission trips, and she may develop a long-term interest in spreading the gospel overseas!

Full Circle

The ultimate goal is to help your daughter become so skilled at goal setting that it seems natural for her to turn around and help her friends—and eventually her own children—set and meet personal goals.

So Many Choices

But along with setting reasonable goals comes the responsibility of making wise choices. During your daughter's childhood, chances are you made most of her decisions for her. As a little girl, she depended on you to help her decide what to wear, what time to go to bed, and how long she could play outside.

But as she reached her teen years, you probably realized the need to give her a little more freedom in decision making. With that freedom, however, came the responsibility of learning how to make wise choices. Guess what? Your twenty-year-old daughter is still in the learning process when it comes to making smart decisions.

Granted, she'll make some light decisions that may not seem to have much weight, such as which color of shoes to purchase or whether to apply blue fingernail polish or green. But as she matures, her options will gain more weight each year—everything from whom she'll date to where she'll attend college, if she'll complete college, if she'll do graduate work, how she'll spend her money, where she'll live, how she'll use her free time, and eventually what she'll do with her life.

We Need a Strategy

How can you teach your daughter to make wise choices? First, help her realize that the decisions she makes will determine the direction of her life. Memorize Proverbs 2:9 together: "He shows how to distinguish right from wrong, how to find the right decision every time" (TLB).

As a parent, you'll often know when your daughter is making a bad decision. You could simply *tell* her—but that probably won't have the effect you want. So instead of *telling* her, let me challenge you to *teach* her how to test the decisions she's making. This way, she'll know herself if she's making wise choices.

The Plan

Here are five principles to use to test a decision:

1. The Ideal Test: *Is the choice I'm making in harmony with God's Word?* We're guided either by the world or by the Word of God. Though the world's views are constantly changing, God's Word never changes. There is no guesswork with God's laws. The Bible is our owner's manual. He's the Creator. We're simply the created. We don't have to understand His laws to decide if they're good or not. With His strength, we can accept without understanding. This is the mark of a mature Christian!

2. The Integrity Test: *Would I want everyone to know about this choice I'm making?* Bad decisions often lead to secrets. Are you what you appear to be? A good definition of *integrity* is "when your public life matches your private life." A great verse to memorize with your daughter is James 4:17: "Remember, too, that knowing what is right to do and then not doing it is sin" (TLB). You can fool others for a while, but you can't fool yourself. Based on Romans 14:14, we can conclude "when in doubt . . . *don't*."

3. The Improvement Test: *Will this choice make me a better person?* Let's look at 1 Corinthians 10:23: "You are certainly free to eat food offered to idols if you want to; it's not against God's laws to eat such meat, but that doesn't mean that you should go ahead

and do it. It may be perfectly legal, but it may not be best and helpful" (TLB).

Many choices in life aren't necessarily wrong, they just aren't necessary. If you want your life to count, you have to be focused—and your choices should reflect your choices. Where are you headed? Does your choice reflect God's purpose for your life?

4. The Independence Test: *Could this become addicting?* If this choice has the potential to dictate your life, to control *you*, stay completely away from it. If it dominates your life, it's wrong.

Challenge your daughter to memorize 1 Corinthians 6:12: "I can do anything I want to if Christ has not said no, but some of these things aren't good for me. Even if I am allowed to do them, I'll refuse to if I think they might get such a grip on me that I can't easily stop when I want to" (TLB).

5. The Influence Test: *Will it harm other people?* Here's a terrific scripture to live by: "Yes, each of us will give an account of himself to God. So don't criticize each other any more. Try instead to live in such a way that you will never make your brother stumble by letting him see you doing something he thinks is wrong" (Romans 14:12–13 TLB).

Our goal should be to live with such integrity that if people want to say bad things about us, they'll have to make them up. The small decisions we make develop our character. The big decisions we make *reveal* it.

The Bottom Line

Our choices are really an issue of the heart. If we truly want to make wise decisions in life, we'll submit to God's Word as our base of authority. Want to help your daughter make wise choices?

Challenge her to run her decisions through these five tests. If her decisions pass these checkpoints, she'll experience wise choices and God's very best for her life! This, in turn, will give her more direction for the course of her future.

Analyze It

Has your daughter ever taken a spiritual-gifts test? This can be an extremely valuable asset when trying to decide which direction to head after college. What about a personality test? Again, another essential ingredient to help her realize which careers she'll possibly be most fulfilled in. For example, if your daughter is a people person, she probably won't be happy very long behind a computer inside a cubicle with no interaction. But she'd probably be great as a social director, travel agent, or teacher.

> "Hey, Mom! Let me waste my money sometimes and learn a lesson from it."
> Tobi, thirteen

Has she met with a career counselor? Most colleges and universities offer career counseling, and thousands of students find this useful in securing their niche.

☼ Wrapping It Up ☼

Of course, the most important thing she can do is seek God's will. He promises us in Matthew 7:8 that if we seek Him, we will find Him. And we're also told in the very first chapter of James to take our questions and doubts to God in prayer. I'm convinced that the important thing in life is not "Where can I be the most successful?" or "How can I make the most money?" Rather, the most important thing in a Christian's life is to live in total sold-out radical obedience to the lordship of Jesus Christ. And that changes everything. Suddenly, it's not "What's in it for me?" But our questions become "Oh, Father, what would You like to do with my life?", "Where can I bleed and sweat and serve for You?", "Where can I give to someone who can't give back?"

"I used to never tell my mom and dad anything. I always felt like I was hiding a secret or something. God has shown me that when I share everything with my mom — my conflicts, crushes, concerns — it's way better."

Roxanne, sixteen

If your post-teen daughter is struggling with purpose, meaning, and the right career, I'm convinced the real issue is the lordship of Christ. Will she surrender her dreams, plans, goals, and possible spouse? Will she allow God to break her, remake her, and mold her in His image? If so, the future isn't in question any more. The future becomes the present . . . as in, "Father, use me today to bring glory to You."

Father, sometimes I forget that the real reason I'm even here is to bring glory to You. My purpose in life is not to be successful, or to have a large bank account, or to be well known. My reason for existence is to bring glory and honor to Your name. Help me to instill this in my daughter. Lord, as much as I want her to be comfortable and secure, I want even more for her to be in the very center of Your perfect will.

I love You, Father. And I trust You with my daughter.
Amen.

☼ Memorize It . . . with Your Daughter ☼

For this very reason, make every effort to add to your faith goodness; and to goodness, knowledge; and to knowledge, self-control; and to self-control, perseverance; and to perseverance, godliness; and to godliness, brotherly kindness; and to brotherly kindness, love. For if you possess these qualities in increasing measure, they will keep you from being ineffective and unproductive in your knowledge of our Lord Jesus Christ. (2 Peter 1:5–9)

Shaping a Servant

*How Can We Get Our Daughters to Cease
Being So Self-Absorbed and Tune into the Needs of Others?*

Phyllis pulls a fresh loaf of banana bread out of the oven as her daughter, Amber, runs into the kitchen. "Hi, Mom! Who's the bread for?"

"Mrs. Degaldo," Phyllis says. "I read in the church bulletin yesterday that she's having some tests run at the hospital this week. I thought she could use some fresh banana bread."

Amber wasn't surprised. Seemed like her mom was always taking a dinner to someone ill, baking cookies for visitors at the church, or helping new folks unpack.

> *"I don't like it when my mom tells me that my showers are too long. It's my private time. I cherish it. I have to share a room. Please! Let me have this."*
>
> Tommi, seventeen

"Honey, I've got one more loaf in the oven. It'll be ready in five minutes. I'd like you to help me deliver it."

Amber grabbed her sneakers. Anytime she smelled bread baking, she halfway expected to make the delivery run with Mom. Though she didn't realize it at the time, Phyllis was actually planting seeds of servanthood in her daughter's heart.

Sow Servanthood

At a time when many teen girls are drowning in being self-absorbed, you can change the tide. By directing your daughter's attention to the needs of others and how she can make a difference, she'll be less likely to concentrate on her own wants. Not only will you be shaping a servant's heart, you'll also be guiding her social development skills as well.

How's that? Think about it: No one likes to be around someone who's selfish, absorbed in her own desires, and oblivious to others. *Everyone*, on the other hand, loves being around someone who's genuinely interested in meeting the needs of others. That person becomes a valued friend to many.

How can you develop an attitude of servanthood in your daughter?

Be an example. Because Amber sees her mom exhibiting a servant's heart, it's likely she'll demonstrate the same qualities as well. And since Phyllis takes Amber with her on special deliveries, Amber gets to see firsthand the difference a loaf of bread or a warm casserole can make to someone in need.

Talk about it. Make your daughter aware of the needs of others. For instance, discuss the prayer requests from your church bulletin over the dinner table. If Mrs. Smith is scheduled for a hip replacement, ask your daughter to pray for her. This directs her thinking and her prayer life to include things and people outside her own wish list.

Create a ministry. Perhaps you're not aware of anyone having surgery or needing food. Ask your daughter to help you come up with ideas for servanthood.

Jeff and Kathy teach the young marrieds Sunday-school class at my church. Since their members are healthy and don't spend much time in the hospital, they racked their brains to come up with other ideas of servanthood. While watching their teen daughter,

> *"Mom, don't ask how was school today when I'm still at the front door with my backpack on."*
>
> Amber, fifteen

Kelly, baby-sit, they hit on the idea of offering free baby-sitting for any member of their Sunday-school class once a month.

It's not unusual to see a newborn or a few youngsters at their house with Jeff, Kathy, and Kelly right in the middle of them. They're demonstrating servanthood and giving young husbands and wives the opportunity to "date" their spouse and not have to worry about finding and funding a baby-sitter.

Why Servanthood?

As Christian parents, you'll want to help your daughter develop a servant's heart because:

It's biblical. Ephesians 5:1 tells us to imitate our heavenly Father. Since Jesus Christ served His disciples by washing their feet, and since He served us by giving His life, we want to imitate Him and serve others.

It keeps us from becoming self-centered. The apostle Paul tells us in 1 Thessalonians 5:11 to encourage each other and to build each other up. When we focus on what people around us need, we tend to be less selfish.

It enables others to see Jesus in our lives. And when we think that we "may be the only Bible other people see," it's well worth it!

Conclusion

Now that you've read the book, what are you going to do about it? Will it simply become another addition to your library, or will you respond? Will you move with *action* and *take the initiative* to improve your relationship with your daughter?

A friend of mine with two teenagers in Medford, Oregon, has made a conscious effort to unite her family into a team. Sheri Holtz, her husband, and their two teens have regular family meetings, pray together, laugh a lot, and even have a family cheer. "We call ourselves Team Holtz," Sheri says. "We want our kids to know beyond all doubt that we're going through all of life—the ups *and* the downs—as a *team.*" If her daughter's or son's world should ever crumble, there's no question to whom they'd turn—Sheri and her husband have spent years building a strong, godly support system.

Another friend of mine gets inside her daughter's head—and her heart—by doing a journal together. "It's the most awesome thing we've ever done," Kathy says. "I write in the journal, then I ask my daughter questions and pass it on to her. She takes a week or so, answers all my questions, writes anything she wants to, and usually gives *me* some questions to answer."

They also fill the journal with cartoons, magazine cutouts, poems—anything that is something special they want to share. "One of my most recent entries," Kathy says, "was simply a letter to my daughter telling her how much I love her. I reminded her that as parents, we have prayed for her and her future mate from the day she was born. We're also praying for her career, her character, and the friends she chooses."

Can you imagine the security that gives her daughter? "Our relationship has actually deepened because of the journal," Kathy says. "Nothing is off-limits. She knows she can say and ask me anything in the journal. I started out with nonthreatening questions such as, 'What's your favorite color?' or 'Where would your dream vacation be, and whom would you take?' And in each entry, I always try to include a 'Did You Know' section. And again, that started pretty surface too: 'Did You Know . . . I enjoy shopping with you more than anyone else in the world? . . . I'm proud of your grades. . . . I'm ticklish on my left side. . . . I had a pony when I was a little girl.'

"But now, our questions and our 'Did You Know's' have gotten much deeper: 'What's the best thing about our family?' . . . 'What kind of man would you like to marry someday?' . . . 'What's God teaching you?' and 'Did You Know I regret dating a non-Christian guy during my teen years' 'Are you praying about what God wants you to do after high school? After college?' . . . 'You can ask me anything.'"

Ladies, would a team cheer help restore unity between you and your daughter? Would journaling together deepen your relationship? Are you praying together? How long has it been since you've sat on the edge of her bed? Whatever it takes to establish an intimate, growing relationship with your daughter—do it!

Repeat: Whatever it takes—do it!

Remember . . . your job of raising a godly young woman is unequivocally the most important job in the world!

$\mathcal{E}$ndnotes

Chapter 1: I Don't Understand My Body!

1. Joe S. McIlhaney, Jr., M.D., with Susan Nethery, *1250 Health-Care Questions Women Ask with Straight-forward Answers by an Obstetrician/Gynecologist* (Colorado Springs: Focus on the Family, 1992).
2. Nancy N. Rue, "Tampon Troubles," quoted in Susie Shellenberger, *Everything You Always Wanted to Know About Your "."* (Colorado Springs: Focus on the Family, 1996).

Chapter 2: Preteen to Teen: Making the Transition Easier

1. Kathryn Springer, "Complete Guide to Buying a Bra," *Brio* 9, no. 1 (January 1998): 32–33.
2. Adapted from Greg Johnson and Susie Shellenberger, *Getting Ready for the Girl/Guy Thing* (Ventura, Calif.: Regal Books, 1991).

Chapter 3: Eating Disorders: They Can Eat You Alive!

1. Jennifer Ellis, "Weight a Minute!" *Brio* 8, no. 7 (July 1997): 5.
2. Remuda's Adolescent Eating Disorder Screen was developed by Remuda Ranch and is used with permission.

Chapter 4: Classroom Challenges

1. Angela J. Smith, "Persecution in America," *Brio* 9, no. 9 (September 1998): 21–22, 27-28.

2. This information applies primarily to students in the United States and was adapted from *Students' Legal Rights* by J. W. Brinkley with K. C. Crump (Fort Worth: Roever Communication, 1993). The book *Students' Legal Rights* can be obtained from Roever Communication, P. O. Box 136130, Ft. Worth, TX 76135. Phone: 817-238-2000.

Chapter 5: Classroom Debates

1. Arthur Koestler, *Janus: A Summing Up* (New York: Vintage Books, 178), 185. (Emphasis mine)
2. Stephen J. Gould, "The Return of Hopeful Monsters," *Natural History* 86 (1977): 22.
3. Mark Ridley, "Who Doubts Evolution?" *New Scientist* 90 (June 25, 1981): 831.
4. Paul S. Taylor, *Origins Answer Book* (Mesa Arizona: Eden Publications, 1990), 18, 19–20.
5. Thanks to Joe White, Kanakuk Kamps, Branson, Missouri, for providing information on evolution from his personal research and to Greg Johnson and Michael Ross with *Geek Proof Your Faith* (Grand Rapids: Zondervan, 1995) for providing background on abortion.

About the Author

Susie Shellenberger cohosts *Life on the Edge: Live!*, Focus on the Family's Saturday-night talk show for teens, and is the editor of *Brio* magazine (a Focus publication for teen girls). A dynamic role model for single young women, Susie is the author of twenty-four books, including *Getting Ready for the Guy/Girl Thing* and *Help! My Friend's in Trouble*. She lives in Colorado Springs, Colorado.